Resilience, Gender, and Success at School

AC / SS — Adolescent Cultures, School & Society

Joseph L. DeVitis & Linda Irwin-DeVitis
General Editors

Vol. 1

PETER LANG
New York • Washington, D.C./Baltimore • Boston
Bern • Frankfurt am Main • Berlin • Vienna • Paris

Sue McGinty

Resilience, Gender, and Success at School

PETER LANG
New York • Washington, D.C./Baltimore • Boston
Bern • Frankfurt am Main • Berlin • Vienna • Paris

Library of Congress Cataloging-in-Publication Data

McGinty, Suzanne.
Resilience, gender, and success at school / Sue McGinty.
p. cm. — (Adolescent cultures, school, and society; v. 1)
Includes bibliographical references and index.
1. Women—Education (Secondary)—United States—Case studies.
2. Academic achievement—United States—Case studies.
3. Success—United States—Case studies. 4. Teenage girls—United States—
Social conditions—Case studies. I. Title. II. Series.
LC1755.M34   373.18235'2—dc21   96-44617
ISBN 0-8204-3706-9
ISSN 1091-1464

Die Deutsche Bibliothek-CIP-Einheitsaufnahme

McGinty, Sue:
Resilience, gender, and success at school / Sue McGinty.
–New York; Washington, D.C./Baltimore; Boston; Bern;
Frankfurt am Main; Berlin; Vienna; Paris: Lang.
(Adolescent cultures, school, and society; Vol. 1)
ISBN 0-8204-3706-9
NE: GT

Cover design by Lisa Dillon

The paper in this book meets the guidelines for permanence and durability
of the Committee on Production Guidelines for Book Longevity
of the Council of Library Resources.

© 1999 Peter Lang Publishing, Inc., New York

Printed in the United States of America.

For my parents,

Tess and John McGinty

Acknowledgments

This book was made possible by the friendship and the generosity of five young women from Plains High, Plainstown, Illinois (a pseudonym). They deserve my praise and thanks for their help in its production. The members of the faculty and the administration of Plains High were most welcoming and supportive during my stay. I am grateful to them for sharing so much of their educational work and perspectives with me.

Thanks especially to Professor Alan Peshkin, who showed me the "goodness of qualitative research." He also extended a very warm personal welcome to me and my family during three and a half years in the United States. I would like to thank Associate Professor Lizanne DeStefano, who provided me with a job, opportunities for professional experiences, and friendship while I worked with her. She welcomed me as a colleague, baby-sat for my children, and shared with me her experience of education in America.

Above all, I could not have completed this project without the critical support, insight, and experience of Tony McMahon. I thank him for the hours he listened to me as I talked of nothing but the book, for the many drafts of my writings he read, and for the times he put up with and understood my frustrations and elations.

Finally, I would like to give special thanks to my children, Anna, Tess, and Patrick, as they join those creating multiple pathways to success.

Contents

Introduction

This book grew out of twenty years of educational experience during which I was surrounded by those who were continually asking why so many students drop out of school and college. My question always was, Why do so many with the same sorts of problems and at-risk factors survive and actually do quite well? I believe that a lot is to be learned from those who struggle to succeed at their formal education.

I grew up and went to school in Australia, and from 1980 to 1989, I was fortunate to live and work with Australian Aborigines in rural and urban locations. While living in the remote northwest of Western Australia, I came to know the personal histories of several people and the biography and schooling experiences of one young woman in particular. All of it told to me with some force. I met Ningali when she was fifteen years old and followed her career with great interest. She reframed my notions of success. Ningali inspired me to want to understand in some way the process that brought her from the corrugated iron shacks of her childhood to star in major national and international musical-theater productions.

In these fractured moments in my own life, the point that led to my writing this book, is an attempt to understand the experiences of young women who struggled and compromised to succeed at school, thus creating new pathways to success. Coming to the United States as a participant in an exchange program, and doing the research for an ethnographic account of the lives of young women in a completely different cultural context were exciting and daunting challenges. They made for crossroads in my research experience, moments of decision in which I would review my own subjectivities and examine the ways in which my experiences were being intimately connected with my observations. I make no apologies for this particular view. Diversity observations. I make no apologies for this particular view. Diversity always adds to the rich tapestries of life, and this is another one of them.

Concerning the debate about whether cultural theorists should focus exclusively on social dynamics or become more specific about the contingencies of local settings (McCarthy 1993), this book attempts to weave the discourses of the personal, hence the section on the self-as-agent and the structural critique of the school as an institution.

Chapter 1 gives multiple definitions of success and risk. It also introduces the five young women whose stories form the basis of this work. It samples the worlds of family, school, and work to produce a comprehensive picture of resilience and success. Finally, it gives a critical reading of studies on school success and failure. The readings come from different research paradigms with different premises and are often contradictory in the problems they address and the solutions they propose.

Chapter 2 is a mini-ethnography of the school environment in which the students worked and from which they graduated. It explores the sociocultural makeup of the staff and the students, the politics of the learning organization, and the orientation of the daily administrative matters that kept the school running.

The next five chapters tell the stories of the young women. These stories are told simply and without embellishment, leaving the reader space in which to reflect before moving on to the interpretation that follows. Jackie was a poor white girl whose family circumstances were complicated by one parent's illness and another's temporary unemployment. She worked after school as a full-time gas-pump attendant, and graduated cum laude in spite of much absenteeism. Alexis was the leading African American student at Plains High, a natural leader and very influential in her efforts to improve educational opportunities for other African American students. With great grief and depression, she struggled with family drug abuse and deaths. Sabrina was a special-education student throughout high school. She had a memory deficiency and had been abused as a child. She was inducted into the National Honor Society and was touted as a successful student by the special-education staff at Plains High. Jasmine was a Southeast Asian refugee who had come to the United States when she was five years old. Her mother was on welfare, and Jasmine was occasionally in trouble with the law and was also suicidal. School was her outlet for emotional and intellectual satisfaction, whereas at home she spent long hours alienated her peers and her teachers. She hated school and was often absent. She performed well on standardized tests and was accepted by a prestigious college famous for its theater program.

The following chapter 8 teases out the commonalities and differences in the stories and, where possible, relates them to the commonly held theories of school success. But success for these young women was created by new pathways and supported at three levels: the personal, the family, and the school and the community. These three contexts are then analyzed in the light of the five young women's stories.

Chapter 9 crisscrosses the landscapes of school, family, and community and revisits the influences on success, resilience, and gender. It makes suggestions for establishing school environments that are conducive to success for those who have difficult lives.

The Methodological Appendix gives an in-depth look at the ethnographic methods I used in the research and in the analysis.

Sue McGinty
Townsville, Australia
October 1997

Chapter 1

Young Women, Resilience, and Success

It is May 6, 1992, and Plains High's Awards Night. I sit toward the side of the auditorium so that I will have a good view of the five young women as they receive their prizes for academic excellence. These five young women have been part of this study for the last year. I note on the program that between them they are receiving 16 awards. They are for honors in English, foreign language, journalism, speech, civil rights and human relations, state scholars, and presidential academic fitness. As well, several of their names are listed under prestigious extra-curricular activities. Plains High offers 55 awards for academic excellence.

One of the five young women arrives with her parents and takes a front seat. Her parents are grieving the death of her uncle, murdered the week before in a gang-related shooting in town. The other four young women do not show up.

Later I find out that one young woman was grounded by her mother because she had to go to the police station the next day to be charged with shoplifting. Another said she didn't want to go because she found the last Awards Night offensive. She felt trivialized in front of the crowd when there was no prize after the announcement. "I'm probably oversensitive, but I won't go again." Another was working late and wanted to socialize with her friends afterward, so she didn't take the night off to attend the ceremony. One didn't come because there were no prizes for those in the special-education department. (Field notes)

This book explores how five young women, seniors at Plains High, became successful at school. At the same time, each of these young women had lived with stressors such as poverty, family disruptions, substance abuse, and antisocial behaviors for the greater part of their young lives, stressors that are usually regarded as nonconducive to school success. Two of the young women, before this research was begun, had attempted or threatened suicide; all five were troubled by substance abuse in their immediate families; three were victims of physical abuse, and one was a victim of sexual abuse. Only one young woman classified herself as middle class, whereas the others, in their own words, ranged from, "being on welfare" to "very poor" to "poor" to "average." Again, despite these commonly accepted barriers to academic success, these young women excelled in school.

Resilience and Schooling

It is much easier to find research articles and news commentary on failures in school than it is to find studies like this one, of academic success by those who experience multiple stressors in their lives. Literature on school failure and dropouts has assumed that multiple stressors usually prevent academic success or make it difficult to achieve (Callan 1988; Fine 1986, 1991; McGinty, DeStefano, and Hasazi n.d.; Pallas 1984). Most studies of gender and schools, for example, have pointed to the disadvantages of being female when studying subjects like mathematics in the current school system (Linn and Hyde 1989). Similarly, studies of race and schooling have tended to focus on this correlation as problematic (McCarthy 1990; Solomon 1992). Kline and Short (1991) are representative of researchers who study risk and focus on the problematic. They claimed that the emotional resilience of girls decreases as the students progress through high school and that despair and the loss of meaning in their lives become stressors as girls become more afraid of the future and receive less support from adults; attempts at suicide can result when the stress becomes overwhelming. Kline and Short (1991) believe that the cultural expectations of women, the expectations that they be caring, giving, dependent, and passive, contribute to their loss of goals, dreams, expectations, and ambitions. To strengthen the resilience of young women, and encourage assertive awareness of personal power, these authors suggested supportive counseling.

Recently, however, there has been a move to study risk, resilience, and resistance among adolescent girls (Cohen 1996; Minnesota Women's Fund 1990; Schultz 1991; The resilient woman 1992). A growing literature has emphasized students' strengths in becoming successful rather than the deficits that produce a lack of success. The literature has noted protective-factor research, the self-as-agent, family influences, and the school and its curriculum as positive influences on school success.

Recent protective-factor research has been focusing on resilient young people, those who turn out "perfectly normal" despite a host of problems (Garmezy 1991, 1992; Garmezy and Rutter 1983; Rutter 1984; Rutter et al. 1979). A resilient child is defined as one who has the capacity to cope effectively with both the internal stressors that produce vulnerability, such as autonomic reactivity, developmental imbalances, and unusual sensitivities, and external stressors, such as illness, major losses, and dissolution of the family (Werner and Smith 1982). Wang and Haertel (1995) defined educational resilience in this way: "the heightened likelihood of success in school and in other aspects of life, despite environmental risks and adversities, brought about by an individual's disposition, conditions and experiences" (164). According to Schultz (1991), "Resiliency research seeks to understand why certain children who are exposed to significant stressors do not develop severe psychological, learning, or behavioral problems" (6).

Protective-factor research has focused on the strengths of at-risk populations and the quality of caring and support, high expectations, and opportunities for participation in the contexts of family, school, and society that is needed to protect at-risk children (Benard 1992). This research has identified "attributes" that consistently describe the resilient child as being socially competent, possessing problem-solving skills, and having autonomy and a sense of the future.

The characteristics of resilient children and the protective factors that exist in their environments have been extensively studied by Werner and Smith (1982), Garmezy and Rutter (1983), and Wang and Haertel (1995). Research on children and adolescents with risk factors in their lives has usually focused on the debilitating effects of marital discord, low socioeconomic status (SES), large family size and overcrowding, paternal criminality, maternal psychiatric disorders, or removal from the home by local authorities (Benard 1987). Rutter (1984) found that most children seldom experience all these factors, and of those who do, one-fourth are resilient, showing no evidence of delinquency or antisocial behavior. Werner and Smith (1982) concentrated on the study of supportive environments and socialization factors that increase the possibility that at-risk children will not develop the same problems their parents developed. Their longitudinal study found that a supportive environment during infancy and childhood gives children a sense of confidence and coherence that accounts for resilience in later life. They also found that girls are more resilient than boys because of their socialization (the details of how socialization works are not clear), physically robust children have fewer health problems and are therefore less likely to miss school because of ill health, and children who are socially responsive elicit positive responses from others. This final point, of eliciting positive responses, has been found to work positively in establishing the relationships that resilient children need in order to succeed.

Garmezy and Rutter (1983) showed that a combination of personal attributes and environmental factors support resilience. They identified eight protective factors as softening the effects of risk. They then found that adults who had stressful childhoods but did not develop problems could be characterized by any of the following protective factors: they had fewer and less long-lasting stressors in their lives than did those children who developed problems in later life; they had neither a criminal father nor a schizophrenic mother; they had easygoing temperaments, making parental criticism less likely; they were female; they had opportunities to assume responsibilities in school and thus achieved success; they had success, but not necessarily academic success at school; they had a warm, close relationship with an adult and thus had higher expectations; they were planners with coping skills.

Garmezy and Rutter also found that protective factors form a triad of (a) personality-disposition factors that help children cope, (b) a supportive family environment in which at least one parent allows the child autonomy, and (c) an external support system that provides a model for positive values. They emphasized that human development is a dynamic process and that the human personality is a self-righting mechanism that engages in ongoing attempts to organize experience: the interaction and balance of risk factors, stressful life events, and protective factors are likely to determine the outcomes of a child's life. For the present study, Garmezy and Rutter's self-righting mechanism was found to be a useful concept in analyzing the resilience of the five young women.

A caregiving environment in the school also provides a protective shield (Benard 1991), and students who establish communicative relationships with teachers do better in school than students who don't establish such relationships (Davies 1983; Weis 1985a). Not all teachers are open to this type of communicative relationship, however, many studies assumed that teachers' high expectations produce high performance and that their low expectations damage children's prospects for learning (Rist 1970; Rosenthal and Jacobson 1968). Conversely, in a recent study, Goldenberg (1992) found that a teacher who had high expectations of one child and low expectations of another actually had the opposite effect: the child of whom the teacher had low expectations did well, and the child of whom the teacher had high expectations did poorly. Upon further investigation of these cases, Goldenberg discovered that it was not the teacher's expectations that made the difference but what the teacher did: effective intervention on behalf of the child with poor performance increased her reading ability; lack of intervention on behalf of the child who was expected to do well decreased her reading ability. It was the teacher's intervention that led to success or failure, a finding supported by Kenway and Willis (1990), who cited Dweck (1975) as innovative in locating the dynamic of teacher intervention as a factor in how young people view themselves.

Protective-factor research has been influential in discovering what has been hidden from at-risk research: that many young people who suffer stressors in their lives do perfectly well, and some seem little affected by their experiences. In resilient children who have alcoholic parents and do not develop problems with coping, for example, Werner (1989) found behavioral characteristics that differentiate them from children who do develop problems with coping. These are characteristics of temperament that elicit positive attention from parents: at least average intelligence and communication skills; achievement orientation; a responsible, caring attitude; a positive self-concept; an internal locus of control; and a belief in self-help. Yet the findings of this study, as I will show, do *not* support the statement that young people are "little affected" by their life circumstances. The young women to be profiled here were very much affected by what happened to them, but what they did about those circumstances was what made them successful.

The second factor that can lead at-risk children to success is the construct of the self-as-agent, which proposes that the self is an active agent in the construction of one's success (or failure). How people react to their environment, what opportunities are afforded them, and how the environment is changed by the self-as-agent are important for this study. Important, then, are the questions, how do the young women influence the course of events in which they are immersed, and how are they influenced by those events?

Traditionally, the self has been studied as an entity that has been acted on; that is, researchers have sought to discover what happens *to* people in their success or their failure. Thus, Betz and Fitzgerald (1987) found that girls with higher self-esteem or higher self-confidence tend to have a strong career orientation. But high self-esteem and successful academic performance have not been found to be linked causally, although this link has been implied by some researchers. For example, Pines (1984) said that self-esteem allows some girls to exert control over their lives and avoid disasters such as unwanted pregnancies. The self-fulfilling prophecy, that those who think badly of themselves generally achieve less, has also been extensively examined by Bandura (1977) and Bandura and Schunk (1981). They propose that people learn by encoding what has been observed and by forming expectations of, and aspirations for, their own behavior. All people do not form expectations and aspirations in the same way, however. Children of alcoholic parents, for example, react in different ways to their parents' substance abuse; only 5 percent of female relatives of male alcoholics were found to be alcoholic themselves (Benson and Heller 1987).

In seeking explanations for success in the lives of seven eminent women, Kerr (1985) found key early experiences that she said contributed to their success in later life. The key experiences are having time alone, feeling different, receiving individualized instruction, having childhood mentors, receiving guidance and encouragement during adolescence, refusing to acknowledge the limitations of gender, having an ability to combine roles, having a strong sense of personal identity, taking responsibility for oneself, and having a mission in life. Kerr found that all the eminent women had these experiences in some form and thus had an edge over their noneminent peers. She also examined theories that attempt to explain why women have difficulties with achievement. Explanations include the fear of success, the Cinderella complex, and the impostor phenomenon, all of which concentrate on the personal reasons for the failure of women to become fully actualized persons. She only briefly acknowledged "external barriers," such as societal pressures. Kerr's work, like that of many other researchers (Bandura 1977; Betz and Fitzgerald 1987; Farmer 1977, 1985; Gottfredson 1981; Hutchinson 1985), while acknowledging the part played by others in the success of the women studied, emphasized the importance of personal attitudes and dispositions in achievement and success. In a recent report, Cohen (1996) observed that girls negotiate school successfully by adopting various strategies, such as "speaking out," that is, voicing views freely and openly, thus gaining notoriety, and "doing school," that is, meeting teachers' expectations by being compliant, or by "crossing borders," which means acting as a go-between for students of different cultural groups or for teachers and other students.

Other proponents of the self-as-agent have also stopped short of contextualizing the experience of self. Rosenberg (1974) made the distinction between the self-as-subject and self as the executor-self or the doer-self, and the self as object of one's own knowledge and evaluation. When one is both object and subject simultaneously, the self is reflexive, and a self-concept emerges. Yet Rosenberg ignored the influence of factors other than self, such as culture, ethnicity, and gender. Mills (1991), as well, in distinguishing between the "early theories of motivation based on Freud which assumed that people were motivated by 'drives' to meet basic needs" (67), and more current research, which has "produced a new metacognitive self-as-agent" (68), defined self in terms of "being the source of an innate inner wisdom and uncontaminated state of well-being." According to Mills, "This wisdom is recognized in day-to-day life as what is normally called 'common sense' or insight. It is the source of creativity and invention and the source of higher-order feelings such as the joy of discovery and of unconditional well-being" (69).

Mills believes that this higher-order self is independent of past experiences and has direct implications for the practice of counseling students in stressful situations. For example, a lot of attention has been given to programs to enhance the self-esteem of women. Yet this discourse on self-esteem, including Mills's, has ignored or repressed matters of culture, identity, and power, which are important points, since self-esteem programs that are based on negative self-images are doomed to failure. This criticism of self-esteem programs has also come from Kenway and Willis (1990), who found no evidence that girls suffer from low self-esteem. They stated that the real problem may be located in social practices rather than in individual self-concepts, and they would criticize Mills for disconnecting the social from the individual in the development of self-esteem. The myth that motivation is all that is needed to succeed at school is strong. In contrast, McCaslin and Good (1992) pointed out that structural support can make all the difference in enabling students who have potential but poor backgrounds to make educational progress: "Students need many models to help them understand what they do not know and how to make progress . . . they need help in understanding their emerging ideas and they need people who simply look out for them. . . . Effort is not an individual variable" (10).

The external environment, therefore, is crucial in developing a concept of self. The idea of the self-as-agent developing not alone but in context or in community was explained by Benhabib (1992):

The human infant becomes a "self," a being capable of speech and action, only by learning to interact in a human community. The self becomes an individual in that it becomes a social being capable of language, interaction and cognition. The identity of self is constituted by a narrative unity, which integrates what "I" can do, have done and will accomplish with what you expect of "me," interpret my acts and intentions to mean, wish for me in the future, and so on. (5)

Locating the self in the myriad social contexts or in a "web of narratives," as Arendt (cited in Benhabib) emphasized, we are both author and object of our own life stories:

A coherent sense of self is attained with the successful integration of autonomy and solidarity, or with the right mix of justice and care. Justice and autonomy alone cannot sustain and nourish that web of narratives in which human beings' sense of selfhood unfolds; but solidarity and care alone cannot raise the self to the level not only of being the subject but also the author of a coherent life-story. (198)

Smith (1987) spoke noting the implications that research on the self-as-agent has for women: "A sociology for women preserves the presence of subjects as knowers and as actors. . . . The standpoint of women therefore directs us to an 'embodied' subject located in a particular local historical setting" (105, 108). Thus for this study, researching the standpoint of the five young women meant doing research that made a space for their contextualized voices in the everyday worlds of home and school. This approach acknowledges that the environmental influences that have an impact on the self can either destroy or help create success. The task is to understand how the young women act and how they are acted upon in the settings that surround their lives at home and at school. What agency can they bring to an institution like the school or the family, and how do they experience that agency in the school and the family?

The third factor that can lead at-risk children to success is family influences. Families are the starting point in all biography (Denzin 1989b). How they contribute to the success or the failure of their children has been attributed to such differentials as disciplinary and parenting styles, SES, the possession of cultural capital, and class lifestyles. Families are thought to have enormous influence on a student's success at school (Baumrind 1978; Clark 1983; Hess and Holloway 1984), and the extent of this influence has been predicated on the fact that "American education is structured to serve children who have had the average family experience or better" (Corner 1988,

28). What happens to those who do not have this "average family experience" has usually been categorized with the problematic aspects of education, such as dropping out of school. Contradictions to the "norm" provide researchers with an opportunity to see what is different from the stereotypical images of failure or success.

Research has shown that families influence the ways in which young women become successful. There are studies that support the more commonly known indicators of success, such as high SES, professional parents, and active involvement by parents in their daughters' education, and there are studies that look at the problems of race, class, and gender as they relate to educational achievement. Clark's (1983) study found that no matter whether the family units comprise one or two parents, are wealthy, or are welfare recipients, those with successful children have authoritative parenting styles. These parenting styles are warm yet provide rules and regulations and so lead the children to secure and trusting relationships that are transferred to the school setting. Steinberg, Elmen, and Mounts (1989) supported the finding that authoritative parenting leads to success in school. In contrast, Clark also noted that the families whose children are low achievers in school have authoritarian (dominating and demanding) or permissive (inconsistent) parenting styles. Children in such families display a greater degree of despair, pathos, lethargy, and psychological confusion than do children from homes with authoritative parenting styles, and they transfer these characteristics to the school setting.

Earlier studies supported the notion that a high degree of parental support and tight control result in academic achievement (Baumrind 1968, 1978). Clark's (1983) study of poor black families refined the findings of Baumrind (1978) and Rollins and Thomas (1975) by making the distinction between toughness generally and toughness in regard to academic achievement. Subsequently, Kotlowitz (1990), for example, found that a young boy in a Chicago ghetto wanted to do well in his spelling because the achievement gave him a sense of personal satisfaction and because his family, especially his mother, was very proud of him. Clark believes that the lessons of learning to be tough or resilient in the ghetto can be translated into academic achievement, and Marston et al. (1988) found that teenagers who are apparently invulnerable to drug, alcohol, and nicotine use claim to have better health, more successful social relationships, and a happier state of mind than teenagers who use these substances. Nonusers also report a lower incidence of problems among their parents.

Some research has noted that boys and girls develop differently in similar situations. Rollins and Thomas (1975) stated that girls are socialized in a different way from boys and that the toughness girls require for academic success is likely to result from authoritarian parenting and a lack of support from parents who exercise a high level of control. Yet Callahan (1991) believes that a preoccupation with differences between the sexes leads to speculation about biological determination even though no evidence has ever been found to support such a theory. Middleton (1987), in an analysis of family and school, showed that the creation of cultural capital (the knowledge that children acquire from sources other than the school that enables them to survive in society and succeed in school) is fraught with contradictions. She showed that family dynamics produce, for example, the sexual division of labor that also operates at school. All three women she studied were successful, but all were critical of their early socialization as females, which they claimed, promoted the sexual division of labor. Middleton said, however, that one of the factors in their success was that they did have access to the resources that provided them with the know-how to be successful in the formal system. Having access to resources wherever they exist is clearly important to success.

Other research linking families to school success has shown that college degrees held by parents confer educational, status, and economic benefits on their children (Gruca 1988). Working mothers have been found to encourage higher educational aspirations in their daughters than nonworking mothers (Bergquist, Borgers, and Tollefson 1985), and fathers have been shown to influence significantly a girl's choice of a nontraditional career (Wilson, Weikel, and Rose 1982). These predictors of success will be challenged in the case studies presented later in this book.

Schools have been advocating parental involvement in their children's schooling for some time, but Fine (1991) believes that this advocacy has not been effective, leaving working-class parents at a loss to ensure their children's success. Fine spoke about the fear with which many parents approach school for whatever purpose and the continuing fear of "what will they do to my son or daughter when I leave here?": "Negotiations . . . dramatically reveal the social dynamics of race, class, and gender that undermine the one public sphere in which mothers believed they could make things better for their children" (164).

Studies of social class have shown the educational advantages of being middle or upper class and the difficulties that the working class or the lower class and welfare recipients have with schooling. Gottfredson (1981) found social status an influential factor in predicting the level of occupation to which a person aspires. She also found that lower-class persons have foreshortened horizons and, consequently, limited career aspirations. While most researchers have explained their findings by saying that SES is not on its own a predictor of success or failure, Beasley (1988), for example, concluded that students of low SES tend to value goals extrinsic to the educational process and view school primarily as preparation for a job. Weis, in her classic, *Working Class without Work* (1990), studied a high school in an industrialized area where many of the students' parents were unemployed. In contrast with Willis (1977), who found that schools reproduce the classist and sexist society from which students come, Weis found that troubled economic times motivated many young women to stay in school; the girls did not want to drop out and thereby reproduce the poverty of their parents. Weis showed that girls reject the view of women as "less than" that white boys hold and look to the importance of earning wages for themselves as a means of controlling their own lives. She also found, however, a marked similarity among the students in their disengagement from school, even though some were academically successful.

The view that working-class ways of life lead to a lower value being placed on education is, in fact, wrong (Connell et al. 1982). The judgment that working-class parents place a lower value on education is made because of the parents' inability to express a point of view (Fine 1991). Connell et al. dismissed the findings supporting the notion that working-class parents have lower educational expectations of their children. Most research that has asked working-class persons about the value they place on education has found that they rate it highly even though they may have had bad experiences with schooling. They may even rate it highly when they do not know how to manipulate the system to get the best for their children. But whereas most studies have linked success at school with the alignment of values at home and at school, the research described in this book challenges that finding.

The final factor that can lead at-risk children to success is the influence of the school and the curriculum. The term *curriculum* is used in the broad sense of meaning all the activities that take place in the school as well as the atmosphere. In the 1970s, Rutter, one of the most influential early researchers on the effects of schooling on children, went against the commonly held opinion that schools did not matter, saying instead that schools have differential effects on success and failure. Rutter et al. (1979) described the differences between good and bad schools in terms of providing positive, protective environments for at-risk students. The crucial difference is to be found in the school's atmosphere and social organization, both of which are part of the curriculum. The opportunity for students to participate, take responsibility in school, and undertake an academic curriculum are some of the factors Rutter (1984) found to be positive influences.

Powell, Farrar, and Cohen (1985) asserted that a successful school experience is shaped by five key factors: advocacy, which is pressure from inside or outside the school by people who know the system; selective admissions; restricted choices for top students; adult guidance in students' choice of subjects; and high-caliber teachers in advanced classes. Students who have supporters among the teachers and who qualify for advanced classes are at an advantage. In terms of what is taught at school being a factor in the success of young women, Frame (1982), New Zealand's prominent author, said in her autobiography, "I have often wondered in which world I might have lived my 'real' life had not the world of literature been given to me by my mother and by the school syllabus" (215). Frame grew up in a welfare-dependent family. She sought inspiration in what the school had to offer her—literature. For Frame, the curriculum was a liberating experience, but such reflections on the curriculum as a positive influence are hard to come by. Gilbert (1989), for example, argued that most literary analysis in schools supports the prevailing personalistic and individualistic discourse, which does not offer women positions of authority. This literature argues that curriculum and schooling make it difficult for girls to succeed at school.

McCutcheon (1988) discussed the effects of the hidden curriculum—stereotypical messages about minority and ethnic groups and gender roles—that are implicit in teachers' actions and words. The effects of the hidden curriculum can be the perpetuation of gender and racial bias. Eisner (1979) remarked that schools have a null curriculum. By this term, he referred to the curriculum students do not have an opportunity to experience because of a deliberate policy of exclusion or the lack of resources or time.

Gaskell (1985) wrote of students' choice of classes as an outcome of tracking (the system of placing academically similar students in the same class): "There is a good deal of evidence that class, ethnicity, race, and gender are related to the courses students take" (48). Despite the constant criticism of tracking, schools are reluctant to give it up. In an article circulated to teachers at Plains High by the state board of education, the practice of tracking was openly condemned. The writer pointed out that tracking hurt more than it helped and that it benefited no one, least of all the lower-track student. The board said that it disseminated articles such as these to stimulate discussion and thought about the best practices but that the articles didn't necessarily represent its policy.

Schools and curriculum can make a difference in the lives of students (Rutter et al. 1979). The literature on gender issues and schooling has indicated that girls' experience of schooling can be influenced by the messages that the "gender regime" perpetuates, but the ways in which students respond to this regime is more important in gauging success than the negative effects of the gender regime. Successful schooling is shaped by students' positive relationships with teachers. That is a finding of this study.

Success at Plains High

Plains High (a pseudonym) is a large midwestern high school serving a diverse community that includes a university, businesses, factories, and many other commercial centers. Success means a lot at Plains High: "Because of the success of this school, Plains High is the school of choice for parents in this area," said the principal in a talk to parents at an open house in September 1991. The school motto, "Let us boldly pursue success and excellence for all" is printed on the bottom of the daily bulletin, displayed on bulletin boards around the school, and frequently referred to in talks by the principal. The school report card for the 1990–91 (Illinois Public Law 84–126 requires all public school districts to report on the performance of their schools and students in school report cards) school year reported a 92 percent graduation rate, and "*that* [graduation] is the criterion for success at this school," according to a personal communication from a dean of students (personal communication in October 1991).

The school's honor roll is in fact its major criterion of success. For each term, students who maintain a grade-point average (GPA) of 4.0 or above on a 5 point scale are placed on the school honor roll, given a slice of pizza from a local fast-food store, and have their name printed in the school newspaper, which is sent to all students' parents or guardians. Students who maintain a GPA of 4.5 or above from their sophomore year on may join the National Honor Society, a more prestigious honor, as it brings with it the possibility of lucrative scholarships to prestigious universities.

The teachers at Plains High have different views of what constitutes success. There are those who judge success by the students' perceived efforts at school and the way they seem to be perceived by others. A male English teacher said, "Kids who are focused, who have a desire to learn, they are successful. A successful student is one who feels a sense of high self-esteem and is actualizing their potential. I would say that being successful is being seen as effective and being regarded by your peers." Yet a female sociology teacher could look at the gendered context of young persons' lives and question whether success for boys and girls is really the same thing:

> I'm not sure that within our culture we really want to define success as equality. But I guess [girls] are caught in the middle of changing cultural expectations. Many of the working-class girls' mothers did not go on for education, and they may still be in the home. A lot of the mothers we see in the workplace are there of necessity as a result of single-parent situations, and there is a message when I am in the workforce as necessity rather than as a professional choice. Girls are sorting through what it means to be a success. And so I think they are caught. The whole cultural phenomenon of blonde jokes may be a cultural backlash on what success has been. Or does it mean that I am a success if I am beautiful?

A male technical arts teacher saw school success as a result of a family's socioeconomic context: "What makes the difference between success and failure is parental support. If you look at the big picture and if economics contribute to parents being unable to provide a tutor for a child in need, then economics play a large part as to why parental support might not be there."

The five young women in this study were recommended by their teachers and their peers as academically successful students. Personally, they grappled with being labeled "successful." It was not a label they thought of when asked to describe themselves. They knew that they had done well on their GPAs, and all except one had a score higher than 4.5. Three were very involved in extracurricular activities; two were not. All received prizes, awards, or acknowledgment for their leadership, scholarship, or effort.

Kerr (1985) questioned a view of success that relies on tests. She reported that when she interviewed successful and gifted women from around the country, they challenged her patriarchal notions of success as measured solely by tests, occupational status, and salary. She said that because of this challenge, she redefined her use of the word *achievement* to mean "the use of one's gifts and talents to the fullest" (iii). Furthermore, she wrote, "Achievement then is not tied to grades or salary, but to the woman's potential; not to a particular environment, because a woman can operate at full tilt and peak capacity in many settings; not to academic honors, titles, and offices, since these are by-products or signs of achievement, but are not equivalent to achievement" (iv).

While there is some sympathy for this position, the definition of success used in this study embraces the definition of academic success at Plains High—that is, having a GPA of 4.0—and, taking up Kerr's admonition to include factors other than GPA, the recognition of success conferred by teachers and peers. Although this study focuses on the young women themselves, it places them firmly in the context of their daily lives and their school.

Standpoint epistemology (Harding 1991) locates the starting point for research in the lives of whoever is the focus of the research. Biography is the beginning, from which an understanding of success at school will grow (Aptheker 1989; Denzin 1989b). But biography is not enough on its own. It has to be located in the social relations experienced at home and at school. Biographies are multi-faceted stories and perceptions. Smith (1987) said there is a dilemma in having many stories because we must choose whose story to accept as the real one. Do we privilege the powerful with the right to determine whose story is acceptable? Do teachers' or administrators' perceptions have primacy over the young women's stories? Harding (1986) said we have to learn to live with the intrinsically many-sided nature of reality without claiming privilege of one side over another. In this study, however, primacy has been given to the stories of the young women. They were the ones who collaborated most closely with the researcher to provide her with an understanding of success in school.

In undertaking research such as this, I place myself among the growing band of researchers who want to give voice to those who do not perceive themselves as belonging to the mainstream of society, those on the margins. Young women who are successful in school and who experience multiple stressors in their lives are among those who perceive themselves as skirting the margins of the mainstream. But a focus on their lives brings their diversity to the mainstream, enriching the fabric of those classified as "successful." The lives of young women need more explication, particularly in complex situations. Only by crisscrossing the landscapes of their lives can the question of how they become successful be understood in some measure. *Understanding* is different from *explaining* in the objective meaning of the words. This research is not an attempt to find causal factors that predict success but, rather, an attempt to understand the circumstances of these young women's lives at school and at home that they have created in response to the environment in which they live. The dialectical relationship between self and contexts is what I am trying to understand. To do this, I viewed research as a collaborative act (Reinharz 1992) and so invited the young women to be collaborators rather than subjects.

Chapter 2

The School

When you walk through the front entrance of Plains High, you see the bronze letters of the school motto, "Let us boldly pursue success and excellence for all," prominently displayed at the top of the steps. This motto was chosen by the staff in 1987 as part of a conference on planning for the future. It represented the vision that the staff had for the rapidly changing population of the school. Various symbols of success are displayed around the school. Along the corridors, in glass cases, are the sports trophies. A sculpted outline of an Olympic gold medalist, an alumnus of the school, stands in the courtyard. In each hallway are glassed display cases set into the wall. These display cases are the only place where students' work is shown outside the classroom. In one physical-education (PE) display case, a sign reads, WORKING TOGETHER IS SUCCESS. In another, a quotation from Malcolm X exhorts, EDUCATION IS OUR PASSPORT TO THE FUTURE, FOR TOMORROW BELONGS TO PEOPLE WHO PREPARE FOR IT TODAY. In the same case is a hand-printed quote from Frederick Douglas': IT IS IDLE, A HOLLOW MOCKERY FOR US TO PRAY TO GOD TO BREAK THE OPPRESSORS' POWER WHILE WE NEGLECT THE MEANS OF KNOWLEDGE WHICH WILL GIVE US THE ABILITY TO BREAK THIS POWER. GOD WILL HELP US WHEN WE HELP OURSELVES.

Plains High is a relatively new school situated in downstate Illinois in Plainstown (a pseudonym), a city of approximately 65,000. The school was set up in 1963 as an annex of the other major high school in the city. In 1966, according to the *Student Handbook*, the name Plains High was given to the school, and in 1967 a full-fledged high school program was offered. Plains High has approximately 1,300 students in four grades, nine through twelve, and about 114 members of faculty and staff. Culturally the school is diverse, with 23 percent of the student population African American and 4 percent Latino or Asian.

Many of the African American students are bussed from the northern area of town. The other high school in the district has a similar ethnic mix. The principal outlined Plains High's population in this way, "This school serves an extremely diverse group. While other communities have diversity, [Plainstown] has the extremes of that diversity. It has the very, very wealthy, the extremely poor, the very liberal, and the very conservative. It also has a very diverse ethnic population."

Plainstown statistics show that 17 percent of the population is non-white (Foreman 1992, 16); the school's statistics, however, show that 27 percent of its population is nonwhite, an indication of the changing demographics among the city's younger people. Because the school serves this younger population, changing demographics have an impact on the school before they have an impact on the wider community, but the development of diversity at Plains High was not envisaged when the school was established. A veteran teacher said that he thought the school was "originally set up to serve the new white residents of the area and to move their children away from the blacks, who lived in the northern part of town." Many African American students believed that there was still a lot of racism among the teachers and students at Plains High; black-on-black violence was also of concern to them. As Peshkin (1991) found in California, "plans for multiculturalism or ethnicization are not explored and rejected as unworthy, they are ignored" (278).

In order to understand the development of Plains High's philosophy of "success . . . for all" over the twenty-five years of its formal existence, one must to look at significant events in its history. One defining moment occurred during the race riots of 1971. A cutting from the local newspaper from that time describes the events:

> A racial clash involving some 200 students occurred April 29 in front of the school when white students, armed with baseball bats, chains and belts, confronted black students who had been bused to the school. The melee ended with the school being closed for three days, at least four persons injured and 48 students suspended. The incident resulted in an investigation by the City of [Plainstown] and the [Plainstown] Human Relations Commission. No recommendations for expulsion were made and no criminal charges were brought against students involved in the incident. (*The News*, December 31, 1971)

There were charges that the head of the Plainstown Police Department had been derelict in responding to the situation quickly, but the charges were dropped after conflicting evidence was presented. The removal of the principal was called for at a meeting of African American parents who believed that they should have been called to staff the hallways, not the police. In a statement issued through the office of the school superintendent, blame for the incidents was placed on "underlying community prejudices":

Although the principal began procedures designed to prevent future troubles, the school erupted once again Nov. 10 with a melee in a hall in which two assistant principals and one teacher were assaulted. Thirty-nine black students were suspended as a result: eight were recommended for expulsion and two were expelled by the school board. . . . The most significant effect of the incidents, which brought in police to patrol the halls, was that the principal was relieved of his duties and the assistant principal was appointed acting principal. (*The News*, December 31, 1971)

The impact of these events was lasting. In speeches, given by six senior teachers at their retirement dinner, frequent reference was made to the riots of the 1970s and their impact on the teachers' lives. The current principal put the situation in context:

When [Plains High] opened its doors in 1967, there was one black family living outside of the north of the city. It was a very segregated community. Neither the school nor the school district did anything to accommodate or welcome the students who were going to be bused in. In fact, I don't honestly know, but maybe they weren't really welcome. Perhaps that was why nothing was done to make them feel welcome. On the national scene at that period of time, there was a growing sensitivity to race relations, and various kinds of public protests occurred throughout the U.S. The same things were happening in school. I became principal at that time, and there were a number of things that had to be done. But that was a turning point for the school and the community.

The acceptance of diversity is *the* ongoing challenge for Plains High. At the school's 1992 midyear staff in-service conference, the district superintendent spoke to the assembled staff and faculty members about the changing demographics of the district's schools and painted a picture of what they could expect in the next twenty years, given the predicted changes in American society:

Schools will have more ethnic diversity, and by the year 2000 one in three people in the United States will be nonwhite. More students will come from single-parent homes with backgrounds of poverty and therefore more educational problems. The trend for the wealthy is to opt for private education.

The philosophy of Plains High, combining success and inclusion—a philosophy shaped by the racial confrontations of the past—is endorsed by the principal:

> We have worked very hard at creating a school that says that everybody—all students have a place here. We want to build programs in which all students could achieve success. . . . In contrast with the private or parochial school, where there is a more cloistered setting, we've created a climate where everyone is welcome, and there is a place for everyone.

In contrast, teachers often pointed to the fact that providing "success . . . for all" was necessarily limited because the school was underfunded. Funding for Plains High is drawn from the real estate taxes of homeowners in the school district, less than 20 percent of whom have children in school. Teachers believe that a referendum to increase taxes for education will not succeed because of that. The annual operational expenditure per pupil was $4,324.14 in 1992, one of the lowest rates for middle-size high schools in the state of Illinois. The school report card for 1991 stated that the average expenditure per pupil in Illinois was $4,808. Teachers at Plains High envied wealthier suburban schools and their per pupil expenditure and equipment advantage but believe that they are not doing badly considering the low per pupil expenditure. "Our grades on standardized tests compare favorably with those of the richer schools," said one English teacher.

Besides funding, another factor commonly touted as influencing the quality of education is the student-staff ratio. Although the ratio for Plains High is listed as 9:2 (as stated by the school board during cut-back hearings), most classes in the core subjects (math, English, science, and social studies) had twenty-five to thirty-two students. Some of the advanced placement (AP) classes in math and foreign languages and the lower-level core-subject classes had ten to fifteen students. The upper-level English and social science classes tended to have thirty or more students. A senior male teacher complained that less marking of students' work would result in the lowering of standards, and at the same time less contact with students would result in a reduction of students' effort.

> I don't care what research says; class size does affect your teaching. Large classes mean that you do not have time to talk or interact with all the kids because you are always marking their work. Kids love you to take a personal

interest in them, and that sort of contact is connected with success. But it is not physically possible to do it when you have large classes.

There were 114 faculty and staff members at Plains High during the period of this research, 58 teaching members of the faculty and 56 other staffers. In addition, there were 16 special-education specialists, 10 persons in administration, 3 librarians, 5 teaching aides, 7 secretaries, 7 custodians, and 8 cafeteria workers. When specialists are excluded, the student-to-teacher ratio at Plains High exceeds the state ratio of 11:2 (*The News*, March 27, 1990, 17). Plains High had a high student-to-faculty ratio, a fact that did not augur well for individualized attention. Despite the published philosophy of the school as "success . . . for all," low funding and high student-teacher ratios made this task difficult.

The Students

There are official and unofficial ways of describing students at any school. The students' descriptions of themselves are the unofficial perceptions of who's who and who succeeds at school. In most schools, students group themselves according to common interests, race, or SES. At Plains High, there were five major groups (preppies, grits, African Americans, new wavers, and jocks). It was easier for students to classify others as belonging to a group than it was for them to classify themselves. Jackie, one of the five students in this study, gave her perceptions of the preppies while disclaiming membership in the group:

> There are the preppies. They are the rich kids who like to party every weekend. They wear expensive designer-label clothes, are on the student council, and they park their cars up at the north end. They pretend to be friendly, but they're not really. They like going to the country club, swimming on the school team, going to school activities, being cheerleaders, going shopping, and wearing a lot of makeup. They are not as interested in school as a place of learning as much as a place to get good grades and socialize. This group is into success.

Jackie had a few grit friends but stopped short of identifying herself as a grit, though her dress would have identified her as one.

> There are the grits or stoners, who are the kids who like heavy-metal music and smoking. Some of them are into drugs, and they drink a lot. Some in this

group will come to school high as a kite, and they don't care what others think of them. Most of them are not that interested in school. They wear old jeans and T-shirts. They like to make people think that rejection doesn't hurt them. They want to be very tough, and they don't want the rich kids thinking that they are superior. They usually gather on the south end of the school or go across the road to smoke. This group is not into success at school.

Tania, a white student, explained her impression of the groups of African American students in these terms:

If you drive past the school, you think it is all black because that is where the black kids hang out [in the front]. Most of them stay together, but some of them mix, mainly the rich ones. The black kids are sort of not segregated but not together either. Some of them wear expensive clothes and heavy gold chains with wild haircuts. A lot of them don't do well in school because they think it is cool not to achieve.

Shana, an African American student, noted:

I've moved around a lot because my dad is in the military. I've lived in Texas, Kansas, and New York. I've never been told that I can't be friends with this person because they're not black. [But] when I got here, I hear about sellouts and that is a person who's sold out their race. You sell out your race by mixing with white kids or by being successful at school. But I don't understand because you are going to be black no matter what you do. I think this attitude is from girls who are jealous.

From other students, I learned about the new wavers, a small group of students who were committed to band or theater. They wore black clothes and shoes and hung out at the coffee shops around town; some of them smoked cigarettes or marijuana or did drugs. They liked to talk philosophy, discussing life and themselves. The were reported as being more into learning for its own sake than for achieving the kind of success that the school rewards.

The jocks were into athletics.

Apart from these defined groups, there were other smaller friendship groups, students who crossed the boundaries between groups, and a fairly large number of students who didn't easily fit into one of the five categories.

The official student organizations give a different perspective on the school. The student council gives its members an opportunity to participate in school government. According to the 1991–92 *Student Handbook*, "the student council is the representative body for students. Members are elected in the spring to represent different geographic wards of the Plains High school district" (35). The student council's primary aims are (a) to encourage potential leaders to accept leadership and responsibility, (b) to develop within the individual student a sense of responsibility for his or her own conduct, (c) to provide an organization through which students' opinions and interests and desires may be conveyed to faculty members and administrators, (d) to promote school loyalty and spirit, and (e) to encourage students to participate in the affairs of the school.

"Getting elected onto the student council is a real popularity contest," one student reported. "You have to work hard at getting known so that you get the votes." Once on the council, representatives must abide by attendance and participation requirements. Jasmine, one of the young women in this study, was elected to the student council during the year of this study. She didn't talk about it much; it was just another way for her to get involved and be on more committees, a signifier of success. She admitted that she wanted to be popular and to be known.

When asked about successful students and why they thought these students were successful, teachers at Plains High responded that the outward manifestations of success, such as club-officer positions, were usually held by those of higher SES. This presumption was difficult for the teachers to verify unless they knew the parents of these students. When asked what SES the five young women of this study had, teachers invariably said middle class. One senior female social studies teacher said:

> I think in the high school setting there is an awareness that some are not wearing the labels or the ninety-dollar Nikes. In a class that I have this fall, there were tensions arising over social distinctions, and students were defensive about that. I think that working-class girls feel in the middle. Many of the organizations' positions are held by students who, by and large, are from a higher SES—professional parents. Interpersonally and socially, that becomes a pressure as far as working-class girls go. Their jeans won't be the Guess? jeans. But they will be meticulous about their appearance.

Creating the illusion of middle-classness in the eyes of the teachers may have helped some of these young women create a perception of potential success. On the other hand, Jackie's being a grit who was interested in success and in learning made teachers respond to her in a way that was supportive of her interests.

More than twenty-six extra-curricular clubs were sponsored by the faculty of Plains High. These clubs provided for diverse interests: sports and sports-related activities groups like wrestling and cheerleading; cultural activities, such as those provided by the International Club, the African American Club, and various foreign-language groups; social issues and service; the newspaper, the yearbook, and other literary pursuits; music and drama, whose clubs sponsored more than ten public performances each year, including band concerts, choral recitals, and musicals; and the close study of various academic subjects, such as computer science and business. Each club met after school twice a month. Clubs such as the Honors Society held annual inductions and had benefits such as prizes and awards attached to their membership.

The school regarded club membership highly and regarded committee participation even more highly. It was estimated that about one-quarter of all students at Plains High were involved in at least one club; many were involved in several. Most staff members were sponsors of at least one club.

Club membership was important in the perception of school success, especially when students were applying to prestigious colleges. Students with a history of involvement in school clubs were preferred to those without a history. Not belonging to a club could also result in scholarships not being offered, as happened in the case of Jackie. After-school work commitments prevented many students from participating in these extracurricular activities.

The quieter side of support for school success at Plains High was the Counseling Center. The Counseling Center offered group programs and individual counseling to enable students whose fragile lives were in chaos to hold themselves together. The school social worker was a dynamic African American woman with a wealth of experience and excellent cross-cultural communication skills. She trained staff members, counseled students, trained students to assist in the counseling process, and served on innumerable committees throughout the school district and the state. She established several student-support programs that directly influenced the lives of the students in this study.

Many researchers have discussed the positive and negative influences of peers on school achievement. McRobbie (1978) and Willis (1977) claimed that some students resist school authority and form groups that draw once high-achieving students into rebellion against the authority of the school. The students who form these groups delight in regular truancy and low grades, even though some of them are capable of high achievement. Weis (1990) believes that resistance to education was a product of the 1970s, when there were jobs for all, and it didn't matter whether students did well at school or not, for they could always get jobs in the factories where their parents worked. In these days of unemployment and economic insecurity, however, girls in particular are more likely to seek independence in financial matters, and they are more keen on using education as a means of doing that. Yet there is some evidence that resistance to schooling still exists (Solomon 1992), especially among some students in minority groups.

Peer support in a school, in the form of both organized programs and unofficial support, fosters resilience (Legters, McDill, and McPartland 1994). At Plains High, one support network that distressed students turned to was peer counseling. About twenty juniors and seniors each year were trained to offer assistance, encouragement, and support to peers in a problem-solving process. This service was available to students who preferred to discuss their problems with another student, someone who related closely to their problems. Two young women in this study, Alexis and Xia, were peer counselors. Xia, in particular, was often absent from class to serve as a counselor.

Another form of support was peer tutoring, a new program at Plains High. Students volunteered their time to coach other students in the areas of their expertise. Usually this happened before or after school or at lunchtime. In the initial days of the program, there were more volunteers than participants.

Yet another support program was for teen parents. Pregnant girls and sometimes the prospective fathers met regularly to discuss parenting. There was also a home-bound program, which provided pregnant girls with home schooling one hour each weekday during the last month of their pregnancy and in the first six weeks after birth. Girls in this program thought that it was the only way they could keep up with their studies. It enabled one girl to graduate early and continue her studies at a local junior college.

The realities of becoming a parent and continuing in school were generally not so positive, however. As one administrator said, "It is academic suicide to have a baby while at school." The school statistics on girls who had babies and then dropped out support this statement. At Plains High in 1991, only one girl who had a baby was able to maintain a 4.0 GPA and graduate; she gave her baby up for adoption.

The six girls then known to be pregnant were not doing well academically. As one administrator put it bluntly, "The bright ones have abortions."

The perception of academic success at Plains High did not include having a child. The antagonistic attitude toward pregnant students could be seen in the case of Cassie, who was a candidate for inclusion in this study but dropped out of school during the year. She was a bright young woman with a nine-month-old baby, a GPA of 4.2, and an aptitude score (ability test) of 118 with 100 being the mean. She had come back to school after the birth of her baby only to be confronted by silence and indifference on the part of the faculty. She complained that teachers gave her the feeling that having a baby was not the smart thing to do if she was to succeed at school:

> Last year I was gone for about three months. My teachers knew I was gone, and they knew I had a baby. I had a home tutor. She would talk to the teachers and would get my homework for me. She would keep them posted—"No, she hasn't had her baby yet"—so they knew what I was out for. But when I came back, I remember only one of my teachers said something to me about it. She didn't really say anything but "How are you? How's the baby? What did you have?" The other teachers acted like they didn't know anything when they did. They didn't say anything about it; they didn't ask how I was or say "Welcome back." It was just like I was back in the class and "Here's your work."

That said, Cassie laughed.

Cassie intended to stay in school, graduate, and go to college. Her mother-in-law, a university professor in another state, was influential in her wanting to stay on at school, so she had some extended-family support. By the end of the year, however, she had dropped out, returned once for a few months, then dropped out altogether. Admittedly, the stress of having a baby places a different complexity on staying in school. But the response of the teachers was the vital difference between the way Cassie was treated after her pregancy and the way two young women in this study were treated upon returning to school after illness (Sabrina) or after time off to look after a sick parent (Jackie). Cassie had no one to cut the slack for her, and she knew about the faculty's silent disapproval of having a baby while in school.

Thus at Plains High becoming academically successful required more than personal effort; it was allied with the faculty members' and peers' perception of who was successful and what it took to be successful. Becoming pregnant and keeping the baby was not perceived as behavior that enhanced success. None of the five young women in this study had children.

Clarification of whether or not peer pressure influences some girls not to succeed came from two of the top five female academic achievers at Plains High. Susan agreed that peer pressure was a strong influence on some girls not to succeed. In response to the question, she stated:

> Yes, a lot. Some girls say to me, "How can you live without guys?" and that is stupid because the guys they go out with are not even going to go to college and are just watching football in front of the TV with a big beer belly. I want to look ahead of that—a broader span instead of just now.

Loan, another female achiever, supported Susan, but she also believed that to be successful, one had to resist the pressure to be a "flaky" girl. Loan said:

> I think the problem with girls who are influenced by peer pressure is that they don't look within themselves to find approval; they always have to ask somebody else. Does this look alright? Is my hair done right? and things like that. And this annoys me because I say, "Why don't you ask yourself?" I guess the problem is those who want to be popular.

Kessler et al. (1985) believe that a "gender regime" operates in schools and in classrooms. A gender regime is defined as, "the pattern of practices that constructs various kinds of masculinity or femininity among staff and students, orders them in terms of prestige and power, and constructs a sexual division of labor within the institution. The gender regime is a state of play rather than a permanent condition" (42).

A group of female students at Plains High complained that participation in Girls' State (a week of training in government made available to students statewide) was limited: only two girls from Plains High were sponsored, whereas ten boys were sponsored for Boys' State, and this, the female students believed, reflected society's prejudice toward women in politics. Their anger at this unfairness was expressed by Loan:

> It says to boys, "This is an educational experience, and you'll really get something out of this for your future." People really see boys in that role in later life. For girls, it is just fun and tokenistic. So they only pick two to go. Why can't ten girls go, the same as the boys? It means that they don't really consider politics an area that girls will go into. That makes me sick.

Back in 1972, statistics on the lack of resources available to girls in schools were used very powerfully in the arguments that led to the implementation of the federal Title IX Education Amendment, part of which reads, "No person shall, on the basis of sex be excluded from participation in, be denied the benefits of, or be subjected to discrimination under any education program or activity receiving federal financial assistance" (cited in Sadker and Sadker 1982, 39).

Yet, according to Sadker and Sadker, sex bias and discrimination continued to permeate school life. This is most graphically portrayed in the area of mathematics, where many studies have shown that boys are encouraged to study math, whereas girls are discouraged from it (Wilson and Boldizar 1990). The early socialization of girls has been blamed for this discrepancy (Fennema and Sherman 1978). Yet it is difficult to see how the socialization of girls is to blame when sponsorship for Boys' State and Girls' State was so unbalanced. It is the gender regime in operation within society.

This gender regime within Plains High was at work not only among the students. Several teachers pointed out that gender inequality did exist in the school and that it was entrenched in particular areas of school life. Progress toward redressing the inequality was being made incrementally. Female teachers' attempts to teach upper-level classes were successful in two departments. After years of complaints that only male teachers taught AP math and science and that some upper-level students were leaving the school without ever having been taught by female teachers in these subjects, "a threat to lay a sex-discrimination charge against the school helped to get things changed rapidly," a female math teacher reported.

Fennema and Sherman (1978), in discussing evidence that supports the debilitating effect of female socialization, noted that although women are numerically dominant in the teaching profession, they do not occupy positions of authority. The lack of female authority figures is said to influence young women's formation of their career aspirations. Fennema and Sherman also pointed out that girls are conditioned to believe that they are not as intellectually capable as boys, and although teachers reported that they treated boys and girls the same, this claim was not supported when the teachers were observed in the classroom. It has been suggested that the absence of female authority figures is a significant factor for young women who choose traditionally female careers as well as for young women's perceptions of success.

The Teachers

At Plains High, the curriculum is prepared by the teachers in conjunction with state requirements and district regulations. Delivery of the curriculum is the responsibility of the teacher. Whereas there were many examples of ways in which to engage the curriculum, cooperative learning was touted as being particularly effective in facilitating learning in at-risk students (Benard 1995; Berliner and Benard 1995). One teacher explained how she introduced cooperative learning:

> One of the first things we do in the course is we talk about different learning styles and the opportunity to work cooperatively rather than always working individually or competitively. High schools are difficult because kids are not used to learning cooperatively. The kids might say they hate cooperative learning because they have a situation where one person does all the work and the others freeload. But then I point out that they should not allow those freeloader situations to exist. And they get to know who to leave off a team, and that is giving a message.

It was obvious from sitting in on some of these classes that students love working together. One teacher pointed to active engagement in the class as a signifier of success: "We inherit a lot of kids who are not used to working. It is hard work to get them working. Some of them don't care. But those who have been engaged are active participants in their education."

Teachers rewarded engagement and enjoyed it themselves, and thus the cycle of learning was perpetuated. A senior female English teacher said:

> I say to the kids that on the whole this school works, we get along, we live here; it is like the neighborhood, you don't have to go have breakfast with them, but you can live on the same block. My focus and purpose in the school is to stress that school success is getting along in the whole group.

To an observer, cooperative-learning classes seemed to provide students and teachers with an energy and an attention to learning that were not evident in most traditional classes. Competition and conflict were part of these classes; in some ways, the tensions were heightened just because students had more say: students in these classes were often heard challenging their teachers' grading system or demanding attention they thought they should be receiving. Cooperative learning is not widespread at Plains High, but several of the young women in this study were participants in cooperative-learning classes and generally spoke positively about them.

Students also found traditional ways of teaching useful. The five young women in this study had taken classes from one particularly traditional teacher, and they found these classes very profitable: "We really learned something in that class," one of them said. The ingredient common to both cooperative-learning and traditional classes was well-prepared and respected teachers. Enrollments in these teachers' classes were always heavy, and these teachers had high expectations of the students in their classes.

Across the school I observed differences in teachers' expectations on the first day of the school year. In an advanced-level English class, the teacher quickly dismissed reading the rules and regulations, saying, "You've been here long enough to know all this; let's begin the real work of learning this subject." He then proceeded to outline the course requirements and began an engaging lesson on the topic of the day. The students were immediately at work. Comments after the lesson were positive: "I like him!" "He's a good teacher!" "I think I am going to learn a lot here!" Downstairs, the Technical Arts, Level 1, senior class was meeting for the first time. The teacher called the class to attention and said that because it was the first day of class, he had to read the school rules and regulations. The students shuffled their belongings and looked up at the ceiling; others began talking to one another in low voices. Few listened. "Any questions?" There were no questions. The students were permitted to talk for the remainder of the period. Comments after that class were about basketball and what happened during the vacation.

Teachers were respected when they took time to work through problems with students, providing examples of how to do the work. Feeling free to ask questions was an important point for the young women in this study, and knowing which teachers were open to that sort of interaction was also crucial. One math teacher worked examples right through from beginning to end, sometimes making mistakes along the way and expecting the students to correct her. One student reported:

> At first we were too scared to point out her mistake, but I think sometimes she did it deliberately to see if we would say something. She was trying to break our fear of the subject and to teach us to trust our own judgment in the area. She was the first teacher ever to do this.

Some teachers accepted late assignments when they knew that students had a genuine excuse, and they spent hours before and after school helping students make up work. These, of course, were the popular teachers. Many of the students interviewed for this study indicated that their interest in school and their successes were due in no small part to the interest or inspiration they received from such teachers. For example, Jackie said, "The teachers will work one-on-one with you, and that's good. But sometimes they are too happy; they're all over your face. But I think they care for me, and that is something." Jasmine noted that:

> I always thought Mr. X was a good teacher because he was involved in my writing, and that helped. A lot of students like to talk with him after school. He has like a fan club, and obviously he is well liked. He has some annoying qualities that I've noticed over three years, and I'm more judgmental of him now because I think his personality changes depending on who he is with. That's manipulation more than anything else. He's very competitive and very into winning. He likes to work very hard to make sure that you win. I guess that is the way he promotes success, by encouraging people to compete, to try harder, to do the best you can, so that you can win.

These examples of things that worked for students highlight the important role that teachers have in encouraging top performance. Teachers demand respect; some earn it. Students complain when they don't get respect, and some of them grow as a result of the respect that they receive. When students talked about what was good or bad at the school, they often referred to the nature of the student-teacher relationships they had developed as "respect." Alexis said:

> There's one teacher who really knows his field well, but umm, he cannot relate to students our age at all. I got along with him, and I think that is because I took an extra part; I tried to be nice to him. But he gets very angry during class, and he will yell a lot, and he will get right up in a student's face—and that's very intimidating, you know—and yell and scream, constantly ranting and raving and preaching about no sex, no drugs, no drinking, no nothing, you know. It's not healthy, and students are like—they don't want to hear it. . . . I think a lot of students don't do well in his class because he has no *respect*.

So, too, with Jasmine, who felt that a teacher's lack of respect for students was counterproductive:

> I'm reluctant to talk up in this class because I don't want to make a mistake and be made a fool. She mocks you. I wish she would loosen up a bit. It seems that she doesn't *respect* the students; she just cares about teaching them and getting the class over with, but she doesn't care about them personally. At times, I think she tries; she's thinking in her head, "I have to be caring." It is

not a very warm class; everybody walks in and says this classroom is so cold, and I don't think it's just because of the air conditioner; I think it is the atmosphere.

The young women in this study believed that being treated with respect was being treated as an adult. They could not relate to teachers who thought of them as children; that was a lack of respect. Teachers gained respect from students when the students thought that they knew their subject area well. Comments like "She knows so much about her subject, and I respect her for that" were common. For both teachers and students, the matter of keeping appointments was an occasion for demonstrating respect. Several times, teachers did not keep appointments with students who had been told to come to school early or stay late to make up work or take missed exams. On many occasions, the students did not turn up for these appointments either. On both sides, these behaviors were interpreted as a lack of respect.

The respect that students showed teachers was rewarded just as a lack of respect was punished. "Cussing," or using bad language, was not tolerated at Plains High, particularly if it was directed at a teacher. "You fucking bitch!" an angry student called a teacher, then stormed out of the class and ran down the hallway; she was suspended for using bad language. Whereas, for a teacher who raised his voice there were no consequences: "Don't give me no lip. You want to see nasty? I'll give you an expulsion ticket! That's nasty!" Among teachers, respect was usually seen as just keeping quiet. Learning the rules of respect and learning how to break the rules of respect without severing good relationships with teachers was part of being successful in the eyes of the school.

Discipline and *control* were two words that one associated with Plains High. From the moment the first bell sounded, the students were monitored. Administrative staff members stopped what they were doing and joined teachers in the surveillance of hallway behavior during the changeover between classes. Faculty members were assigned hall duty for one period a day. At least one faculty member was present in every hallway during class period. Between classes teachers were required to stand at the doorway of their classrooms, and as soon as the bell rang, they were to close the door and commence class. Any student arriving after the bell was to report to Student Services to receive a tardy slip. The punishment was a detention ranging from twenty to fifty minutes. If students left class during a lesson, they had to carry a hall pass with them. Students not carrying a pass were sent back to their class to obtain one or to Student Services for an interview and possible detention. Each class had an attendance sheet, which was collected at the beginning of each class and entered into a computer. At the beginning of each day, a list of the previous day's excused and unexcused absentees was distributed to the teachers. Students with unexcused absences had to report to the administrators that day and so missed class.

The school's control over the students, especially the African American students, extended to their participation in club activities and sports events. Students wishing to hold an activity within the school had to give several months' notice so that the event could be incorporated into the school's calendar of events. This caused a lot of anger among members of the African American Club when they proposed to hold a welcome dance for new students. They were not permitted to hold it because two weeks' advance notice was not sufficient. Although there were few violent incidents at Plains High, police were brought in and security guards hired for public events such as sports competitions and the African American Talent Show. The only other public event at the school observed to have this level of security was graduation. Before the graduation ceremony, students were warned that when they went to the stage to receive their diploma, any behavior other than walking across the stage would not be tolerated: waving to family members, throwing graduation caps in the air, or making gestures to others would result in their diploma's being withdrawn until a written apology was received. This punishment was enforced in the case of one student who waved to his friends in the audience.

Students were not permitted to wear caps in the school building since the way caps are worn can be a sign of gang membership. Some teachers said there was a real danger of physical violence breaking out, and so security had to be tight. Most building advisory meetings included discussion of some measure of discipline or control that someone thought should be introduced or tightened up. One junior female teacher told me that the secret of control was "to show no fear—students who know that you are afraid of them will walk all over you."

When teachers were threatened either physically or verbally, the offending student was suspended. Punishment was the role of the administration. Teachers sent offending students to the Dean's office, where the administrator determined the punishment and implemented it. Occasionally, a teacher gave an after-school detention in his or her own class.

Strong discipline and control kept the school orderly on the surface and purportedly kept the school safe and under control. One is left with the impression that with a few exceptions, teachers and students generally felt safe at Plains High. McNeil (1986), however, makes note of the effects of over-control:

> When the school's organization becomes centered on managing and control-ling, teachers and students take school less seriously. They fall into a ritual of teaching and learning that tends toward minimal standards and minimal ef-fort. This sets off a vicious cycle. As students disengage from enthusiastic involvement in the learning process, administrators often see the disengage-ment as a control problem. They then increase their attention to managing students and teachers rather than supporting their instructional purpose. (xviii)

There was no doubt that many students at Plains High thought that the school had too many rules and regulations and a regime that was not conducive to the type of success that requires flexibility in relation to stressed students.

The Parents

Parent's involvement in their children's schooling is often touted as a predictor of success. Statistics compiled during the Plains High par-ent-teacher conferences indicated that the parents of A- and B-grade students attended in greater numbers than did parents of students with Cs and Ds. Statistics like these are sometimes used to show the correlation between success and parents' involvement in their children's schooling. The young women in this study, however, did not have parents who were directly involved in the school, nor did their parents come to parent-teacher conferences unless called for.

At the beginning of the year, the Plains High principal held "coffee meetings" with parents of new students. Between fifty and sixty par-ents attended these meetings in 1991. Plains High also had a Parent-Teacher Association, which met monthly. It was attended by about fifteen to twenty mothers, whose concerns were with the social as-pects of the school. They usually organized the postprom activities as well as dances and other social functions. Parents had also been in-vited to join the Building Curriculum Committee, which oversaw de-partmental activities and curriculum innovations. There was, as well, a special committee for Staff Development and School Involvement onto which parents were coopted. This group aimed to promote staff collegiality and school-community relations. Parents, of course, helped out at sports activities and other school functions. The school musicals and plays, end-of-the-year concerts, and talent shows were well attended by parents.

Speaking at the 1991 open house, the principal said, "Plains High is the school of choice for parents in this district." He acknowledged the relatively high scores on standardized tests, the famous alumni, and other success stories that Plains High had to tell. A wide diversity of opinions about the school was held by the Plainstown community. Parents spoken to after the principal's speech variously supported or disagreed with him. A mother who had little contact with the school said:

> I am very happy with Plains High. Personally, I think the teachers are good, and my daughter gained a lot from them. They are dedicated, and all you have to do is ask, and they will give the extra help. Teachers have their hands tied because parents don't support what they do.

Another parent, who was not on any committees and did not attend parent-teacher meetings demurred: "People think teachers waste too much money as it is. They have so many holidays. They're lazy. I don't think there are a lot of good educators. Basically they are overpaid and underworked. They have a part-time job."

At the open hearings on the proposed cutbacks in school expenditures there was solid support for the school. Here parents and citizens in favor of increased taxes spoke strongly in favor of a tax referendum, proposing an increased tax for education. One teacher commented:

> I was, frankly, surprised how supportive the parents at the [hearing] meetings were. Less than twenty percent of residents have kids in school. Given the level of animation at the meeting, there is a likelihood of the referendum passing. But I don't think there is any understanding of the difficulty and demands of teaching outside the confines of the school. Even if there is an acknowledgment that this is one of the most important jobs in our society, the molding of our kids for the future, there is not an experiential understanding. We have had massive onslaught of negativism about our profession.

A general indication of a lack of support for the school came when the school board would not put the tax-increase proposal to a referendum.

End Thoughts

Speaking about success with several teachers recently retired from Plains High, I discovered an uncanny agreement among them about the strengths and weaknesses of the school. One retired male drama teacher summed up the feelings of this group of people:

> There are a lot of teachers who care at that school. That is its greatest strength. And it is an unbelievably organized school. In fact, there is a lot of inflexibility. When you have a neat idea, you have to go through thirty thousand committees, and that becomes so stifling that you say, "Forget it!" There is a lot to be said for spontaneity. High school kids are naturally spontaneous. It is a strength to have a lot of older teachers. They have a lot of control in the building, but on the other hand you lose that idealism and eagerness as you get older. Younger teachers bring an enormous amount of energy and lighten up the school. Many teachers go on learning, which is a great example for the kids. But so many of them committee themselves to death.

And a retired female music teacher noted the perennial dilemma of schooling: "All the attention at Plains High goes to the very bright and the very troublesome. The quieter you are, the more neglected you are. But if teachers pay attention to a kid, no matter how small, they will blossom; ignore them, and they will vegetate."

For the district superintendent, school success was a matter of motivation and effort. On the evening of the school graduation ceremony, the superintendent advised the students, "Believe in yourself, and have confidence. Practice to succeed because confidence is not enough without hard work and sweat." At the same ceremony, the chair of the school board told the students, "Happiness is the most important thing in life, but it has a price, and that is the sacrifices you make as an individual." There was the perpetuation of the myth that if you work hard enough, you will be successful. In this study, the complexities of success will be shown to include not just personal motivation but much more than just that. The administration of the school assumed that it provided "success . . . for all," but the school motto, "Let us boldly pursue success and excellence for all," did not necessarily translate to all groups of students. Between the constraints and the opportunities at Plains High was a belief that making a place for all would create successful students. The next five chapters show how the experiences of five young women influenced their perceptions of success and how these young women went about achieving success in this particular school. The different routes these young women took and the strategies used are layed out in detail. Each story illustrates a departure from the stereotypical concepts of success that emphasize conformity and participation, and, thereby, each story challenges the accepted understandings of success.

Chapter 3

Jackie:
Quietly Seeking an Education

I was seated on the living-room couch, sipping a beer and talking with Jackie's parents above the din of the blaring TV when she arrived home after her high school graduation. Her long, straight fair hair flowed in behind her as she whisked through the door complaining about the dress her mother had bought for the occasion. It was a pastel shade with puffed sleeves. She handed the rose she had received as a female graduate to her mother and disappeared into her bedroom. Her mother was feeling ill, and having to sit on the bleachers during the graduation ceremony had not helped her feel any better. A few minutes later Jackie appeared in an old pair of jeans and a black T-shirt with a yellow happy face on the front. In the forehead of the happy face was a gunshot wound from which blood dripped onto the smile. "That's better," she said as she pulled a beer from the fridge. She returned to the living-room and sat down on the floor, glowing with pride, and said, "That was fun, wasn't it?"

Her father leaned back in his chair and said, "Well that's the end. Six of them have finished school now."

Jackie is the youngest of the six children and the only girl. She graduated from high school cum laude.

Jackie's Biography

Jackie's father left school when he was in the ninth grade and went to work in factories. He later joined the army and served in Europe. Her mother, who emigrated from France as a young woman, graduated from high school and then worked at an army base until she married and moved to the United States. Jackie lived in two houses during her eighteen years, one in the country and one in the city. The family remembered with fondness the large, rural farmhouse where they lived until Jackie was twelve. The city house, which was rented, was on a busy main street. There were usually two old cars parked in the driveway, one belonging to Jackie's brother and the other to the family. Her dad drove the family car to work. Opposite the house was the gas station where Jackie worked at night. She walked to Plains High, about three blocks west of the house.

Jackie and her parents spoke nostalgically of the time they lived in the country house. Her mother recounted:

> We had six children at home, but life was good because we were on a farm. We were rather isolated, and we had all the time in the world to, umm, to do some of the academic things that you wouldn't do if you had neighbors close by because the kids would play with them or something. At one point, our television broke down, and so we didn't have TV for about a year. . . . We did some reading and some nature hikes and things like that, walking on the farm. As you can tell by the house, I have always been interested in Native Americans in books. [The living room of their house is lined with books and pictures of Native American peoples.] On the farm, we found some arrowheads by accident, and so we searched for them, and we would discuss why at one point there would have been Indian camps there. We know from the records that there was. And we would discuss why. There was a little river and natural springs all over there, and things like this.

Jackie's father interrupted this idyllic picture with some memories of his own:

> But times were tough. I was raising six kids, and all I had was a factory job, and I had to drive forty miles to that job. We made it because I raised a big garden plus I took care of a guy's cattle, and that way we had meat, plus I hunted a lot. But we done things together as a family.

The mother continued, emphasizing the importance education had for her, an importance she wanted to pass on at least to her youngest child, her only daughter:

> When the children came home from school, even though they wouldn't have any homework, I would always give them homework—like a page of writing or printing, things like this. They didn't like it, but they did it because I wouldn't allow them to do anything else. I feel the schools here are, uh, so lax. I had gone to France, and I had seen that my brother's son, who was in a grade below one of my sons, was more advanced than my son was, and I realized that that was it. Jackie was the youngest; I had more time with her. We used

gether. It kept her occupied, and I
in't speak to my children in French
onto my children or my husband.

this isolated area, the youngest
with her "forming her personal-

ouse. I enjoyed it, but most people
there. There was no movie theater,
, and a place that sold cars . . . .
e school, but if you were gifted in
and play on his computer: games
n I had there. . . . The books I
the worlds I retreat to, and they
between the covers of a book.

reader, and a lover of music,
heavy metal bands sing about
, which is mostly painful, sad,
etal doesn't hide behind soft
on't mean anything to me."
mas on the farm when some
ived many expensive Christ-
nts as not being so bountiful.

.... .u.. the only thing in which I could do better than my cousins was in education." While times were economically tough, this seems to have been a period in Jackie's life that was rich in intellectual activity and in forming strong ties to her parents. Her father said, "Yeah, Jackie doesn't have any real material values; she doesn't put much on material things. She's more like her father in this way than you think." Jackie's mother saw education as the way to get ahead:

> You have to remember that I come from a country where there is a social scale, although they say there is not; none of the classes mixes. The aristocracy marry the aristocrat, the bourgeoisie marry the bourgeois, and the working class marry the working class—although I think you can overcome that with education.

When Jackie started elementary school, her mother took out loans and enrolled in a private college in the area. During her first year, she lived on campus and traveled home on weekends; in subsequent years, she lived at home, and her husband dropped her off at the college on his way to work. The children did the housework and the cooking when their parents were not home. Jackie said that she did not remember this as an extraordinary thing, but she was not sure whether her brothers resented having to do a lot of housework. After graduating from college, her mother enrolled in graduate school at a large public university downstate. Jackie remembered that once when her mother was returning to school, she stood at the bus stop crying her heart out because she wanted to go with her.

About this time the company Jackie's father worked for declared bankruptcy, laying off its workers. Her father was one hundred days from retirement and pension eligibility. He could no longer afford to keep a second home, so he sold the country house and joined his wife in the university town. Jackie was then in middle school, thirteen years old. Between the father's unemployment benefit and money from the mother's research assistantship, they managed to hold the family together. Nonetheless, the family lost health coverage and other benefits the factory job had provided. By this time, the three oldest children had left home. Jackie spoke of her attitude toward moving to the city:

> I did really well at school that year. I think I got straight As. It was real different. But for some reason, I wanted to do better in the city than I did in the country. I thought that I had to show these people that I wasn't just some country bumpkin. I think, too, the fact that none of my brothers ever studied very hard bothered my parents. To me, children should hold up the parents' honor, and to me the children should do well so that people think well of the parents and the whole family. Well, my brothers weren't doing that. So I thought, "Somebody has to do it, and I'm the only girl, so I should work even harder to show that just because I'm a girl, I can do just as well as anybody else."

Jackie continued her hard work at school and was placed in gifted programs from middle school on. Her father stayed on unemployment benefits while seeking employment. He admitted:

> It was tough because it took about eight months before I actually found two jobs that paid five dollars an hour. I was used to making eleven dollars an hour. Life was tough on them because we didn't have that much. The wife was still going to school, and she was working part-time, but she couldn't find full-time work because she was still going to school. . . . I now have two jobs, and when I started, they only paid five dollars an hour.

Jackie said her father was now working too hard, and she thought that they had grown apart a little because she didn't see him as much. "But his being laid off did give me a realistic attitude. I know that I am going to have to work for what I want in life." She started working part-time as soon as she entered high school: "I need the money—my parents need me to have a job because they can't pay for everything." During her final year of school, Jackie was working at least forty hours a week, from 3:00P.M. to midnight three or four nights a week plus all day Saturday and Sunday. She said, "I used to do my homework after midnight if it was due the next day, or I would do it on the days that I had off work."

Commenting on the effect of these long after-school hours at work, her French teacher said:

> She works a lot of hours. It is not frivolous work. She doesn't fritter her money on clothes. I think there is a need for her to work. But I think it interferes with how she performs as a student. She apologizes and says that she has to work so many hours and that she was unable to keep up with the work. And she always gets it to me as soon as she can.

Jackie and her mother spent many late-night hours talking philosophy, sharing reflections on books they'd read, and discussing world problems. Kerr (1985) found that one of the common factors in the successful women she studied was that when they were young, the women spent time talking with their mothers, establishing understandings that bonded each to the other.

Jackie was perceived by her parents and herself as the one to hold the family together. Her mother often told me how lucky she was to have such a thoughtful daughter. Jackie's mother suffered bouts of depression coupled with back pain, for which she received treatment. She never finished her graduate studies. In Jackie's last semester at school, she stayed home most of January to look after her mother during one of her severe attacks of back pain. Her father also stayed home from work during this time. Jackie's mother's illness meant that the mother was out of work for months. Jackie was her mother's nurse and confidante. The school social worker called to ask whether they needed outside help. "We can't afford that type of help" was Jackie's response.

Jackie often spoke about her brothers as having no concern for their parents. This could have been impatient hyperbole on her part, because I saw some of her brothers and their wives visiting the family when the mother was sick. But Jackie clearly understood her role as that of caregiver. Gilligan (1982) commented on this phenomenon.

> Women's deference is rooted not only in their social subordination but also in the substance of their moral concern. Sensitivity to the needs of others and the assumption of responsibility for taking care lead women to attend to voices other than their own and to include in their judgment other points of view. Women's moral weakness, manifest in an apparent diffusion and confusion of judgments, is thus inseparable from women's moral strength, an overriding concern with relationships and responsibilities. (16–17)

Benard (1992) defined the resilient personality as having the attributes of social competence, problem-solving skills, autonomy, and a sense of purpose. Jackie was tenacious, strong willed, and resilient in the face of the apparent contradictions of being loyal to her family and meeting her own needs. When asked what made Jackie academically successful, her mother replied:

> Her own will. You can lead a horse to water, but you can't make him drink. You can give all the values you want to a child, but if they don't want to do it, they won't. So all her accomplishments are her own. A big share of it is because she wants us to be proud of her. She does it for us, not really for herself.

Jackie seemed very conscious of her role as the dutiful daughter; she and her parents and especially she and her mother formed a close-knit, even autonomous unit. When asked about her friends and their influence on her life, Jackie said she had little support from her peers. She did not relate well to people her own age; in fact, four out of the five girls in this study believed they were more mature than other girls their age. The inability of successful women to relate well to other females their own age was also a finding of Kerr's (1985) study. Jackie often spoke about how young people did not relate well to their parents: "Everyone these days thinks their parents are too strict and don't care about them, and I find that hard to believe." She did have about three or four girlfriends with whom she would talk in the hallways between classes. But because she went home for lunch and worked after school, she had little time to socialize with them and gradually lost close contact with them. She said:

> Yeah, umm, with my, uhh, friends—I don't know if I should call them friends or not—peers is a good word. I might ask them, "How's your dad," but only if

they are very close to me. But if you just walk up to someone and say, "How's your mom?" they just look at you as if you are retarded or something, you know?

Several teachers commented that Jackie didn't seem to have a wide circle of close friends. One teacher said, "I don't know if she has any friends. She's an outsider, I think the most outsider of all my class. She sits apart from the class, and I rarely see her interacting with the others." Another teacher noted that "social things are not important to her. If you were to ask seniors who Jackie was, they would say, 'Who?' So she wasn't in the social scene at all."

Surprisingly, Jackie's mother said, "Her self-image is totally negative," and recounted an incident in which a friend of Jackie's told Jackie she was ugly. "I think we are all kind of sensitive to what people think of us, whether we admit it or not. When they say something so negative about us, I think it hurts so deep, and in her case, it just crushed her. There's no self-confidence."

In her freshman year Jackie had a boyfriend, who she said encouraged her to do well. But she also said he just used her. He was in trouble with the law, and they broke up. Jackie said that because the relationship had problems and she couldn't talk to anyone, she turned inward, although "the sex part didn't really bother me because my parents were very open and understanding." But the advice given to Jackie by her mother indicated a concern:

Mom says you can't always depend on a man. You'll have nothing if he leaves you. Now I am very selective about who I let into my life. I have one friend, but she is too competitive for me. She tries to make me look bad in front of others. So she is not a real friend, just a habit I guess. I have acquaintances, but I never really get personal. I don't like them to invade my space. I feel I have problems with my self-confidence. I'm intelligent, but I doubt myself.

Her mother reinforced Jackie's autonomy by stressing that she could not rely on anyone, especially a man. This reinforcement also supported the mother's and the daughter's beliefs in the value of gaining a good education. Her mother said, "Jackie has good values. I always stress how important education is for a woman because then you are never at the mercy of a man. That was taught to me by my father, who said, 'Get an education so that you are never at the mercy of a man.'"

Jackie lived out her mother's exhortations in her own life. During her last semester at school, she became very close to a young man she'd met while at work. The only time she had in which to meet him was after midnight, when they would spend a few hours together. He'd just left his wife and two children in Arizona just four months before. On the days she did not work, he picked her up from school, and they would talk. This relationship lasted only a few months. Jackie said that she didn't want to get seriously involved because her first priority was her education, and nothing was going to keep her from going away to the private college on which she had set her heart. Jackie rarely if ever went out to parties or socialized with anyone but the members of her family. Yet she sought to get away from her dependence on her parents and their dependence on her. She explained:

> The way I'm going to find out who I really am is by going to college—finding out if I can really make it there. I know that I can make it at the state university—that is nothing to me—but college is, you know. I need to be independent, to not be here all the time. . . . I'm dependent on my family. It is like my whole life is here. This place is my life, and I'm not independent, I'm not myself. I don't know who I am because I am too set in here, I am stable here, and to find out who I really am, I need to go somewhere where I am not stable, where I have to work at it, where I have to find out who I am. Independence is an image; it is not concrete. That is why I want to get there. . . . I need to get myself ready for life, you know, for living, and that is hard to do if you are living at home.

In discussions about what it meant for her to leave home to go to college, Jackie often referred to the "gaining of independence."

Jackie's Schooling

I saw Jackie at school every week during her senior year, except when she was absent, and that was often. She usually wore a pair of jeans, a sweater or T-shirt, and old tennis shoes. Her fine, light-brown hair hung straight down her back. She never tied it back.

She had arranged her schedule so that she spent the first period of each day as a teaching assistant (TA). She had no seventh-period class so that she could get home by 3:00 to start work at the gas station. Jackie always sat toward the back of her classes. All except one of her classes in her final year were teacher directed; that is, the students sat in rows, and the teacher lead the discussion or lectured for the entire period. The exception was her AP English class, where the students sat facing one another in a square and occasionally gave presentations. This was her favorite class.

Jackie saw herself as an adult and liked to relate to teachers as adults. She said:

I usually like to talk to teachers about family. If you don't talk to them about their families, you start not to think of them as regular human beings—you know, like they don't have a family, they just live for this place, and they don't, you know. So it helps me to think of them more as human beings with lives. I like to ask them, "How's your husband or wife?" I think it is important that they know that I'm not just interested in them as a teacher. I've never had a rejection from a teacher that way; no one has ever said, "That's none of your business," not yet anyway.

Jackie was able to relate to teachers as adults and friends, and this enabled her to learn. Those teachers who responded to her in an adult and interested way were those she said were "good" teachers. Those who treated her as one of the group or "as a child" as she put it, she did not regard as good teachers. When asked about the connection between relating to teachers and learning from them, she asserted, "For me it is pretty important because I think the better you get along with someone, the more apt you are to listen to what they say. Also, you don't feel bad about asking stupid questions." Her AP English teacher, a female, noted Jackie's effort to relate to teachers as adults as part of her design to remain focused on her education:

Jackie is very focused on getting everything she can out of her educational experience. She is in school to learn. She is not concerned with grades as such; I think she is concerned with how she feels about herself. She is one of those students who constantly makes eye contact when other students are off task, and she will look sympathetically at me and telepathically let me know, "I am hearing you. You have somebody out here who really cares about the subject matter and who really wants to learn." And there is a communication of "Why do these others have to be such immature jerks?" She is really concerned about knowledge; there is a desire to learn. I think she feels a kindred spirit with some of the authors that we read.

Jackie got angry when teachers did not listen to her or did not believe her. She got angry about the frivolity of her classmates. She perceived herself as an honest person; it was an insult when she was treated as a child and not trusted. The strengths of the school, in her case, lay in the caring and supportive teachers with whom she fostered relationships.

Gilligan (1982) pointed out that milestones in the developmental literature had emphasized separation as an indicator of adolescent development. She challenged this notion for girls and said that the opposite is in fact true: "Embeddedness in social interaction and personal relationships is what characterizes women's lives" (9). It seems that Jackie had the ability to engage teachers in her life, and this resulted in surprising support. Her science teacher, a male, made substantial allowances for Jackie because of her circumstances:

> Last year Jackie had six periods of classes, and then she stayed seventh and TAed for me. She could have gone home. This year she is TAing for me in the first period. She is having a hard time getting here because of her work and her mother's illness. Technically, I should be reporting her absent, but I don't. I think teachers cut a little slack for a lot of kids. I suppose in this situation I am cutting a little more than slack. Jackie is in circumstances that she doesn't have a whole lot of control over. Her family is not well off, and she is trying to earn money. She works three till midnight. That's tough! I'm a little more lenient in this circumstance because she doesn't have a whole lot of choices. She has to do what she has to do.

"Cutting the slack" made life at school for Jackie quite bearable and enabled her to focus on her classes when she was present. Several teachers commented on her focus. Her sociology teacher noted Jackie's single-mindedness:

> She has focus. She has the ability to exclude other stimuli and focus on a very narrow range of things—one topic, one assignment—to the exclusion of others. I think she has done that in other facets of her life. Socially, she focuses on a very small clique of friends or groups of friends and excludes all sorts of stimuli that may be threatening to her. She may have been hurt in her interactions with other people, and she just closes them out. It's not just academics. She does it when she reads, too.

Jackie stood out from the other students in a way that teachers saw as very positive. Jackie was touted as being a skilled reader because she put time and effort into her assignments. And she was not uncomfortable about falling behind because, as one teacher said, "She has had enough success or reinforcers that have taught her that she can catch up. In class, she will share, but only if asked. She is not one to have her hand up saying let me tell you what I know." Her English teacher was also impressed by her:

> Jackie is the most unique kid I've ever come across. Peer pressure is irrelevant to her. She always dresses the same. And I get the feeling that TV doesn't influence her identity. She respects authenticity in others. When one of her classmates lost her mother to cancer, she wrote a poem to her because she couldn't talk it out. I think she has acquired her writing skills through her reading and writing.

Jackie said that she didn't like to be wrong when she attempted to reply, and that was a reason she didn't speak out in class. She was also very stubborn, and together with focus, that made her a tenacious learner. Her teachers seemed to have formed a favorable impression of her because of her focus and the care she bestowed on her mother. Her English teacher again:

> Jackie is a very complex young lady. There is a calmness, a presence that is unique, and she is very comfortable with that. She doesn't attempt to change her hair color or her clothing, and she is secure in who Jackie is. That is beautiful because you don't often see that in high school. Maturity-wise, she is beyond most of the students in this class. She was out of this class for a long time with the illness of her mother. Her mother takes medication for depression. She talks about her mother as if her mother was a child that she has to look after and protect, which is very mature for a seventeen-year-old. I think her mother has made her a non-1992 teenager.

Jackie was recommended for this study by a teacher who said that she was successful but did not fit the usual image of a successful student. She was involved in no extracurricular activities, she rarely spoke out in class unless she was drawn out by a teacher, and she had a GPA of 4.6. She was eligible to join the National Honor Society but refused to do so, saying that those sorts of honors were not important to her. She ranked 19 out of 315 in her grade, placing her in the top 6 percent. In 1992, she was listed in the *Who's Who among American Students.*

Jackie scored high on both the Scholastic Aptitude Test (SAT)—verbal, 620; mathematics, 520, out of a possible 800 in each—and the American College Testing (ACT)—English, 26; mathematics, 24; reading, 33; science reasoning, 25; composite, 27, out of a possible 36 in each category. Her aptitude score on another series of standardized tests was in the 121 to 128 range. These scores made her eligible for various scholarships to prestigious colleges. She set her heart on going to the private liberal arts college her mother attended as an undergraduate. The college offered Jackie $15,000 of the $17,000 needed to cover the first year's expenses. She was to find the last $2,000 or send the college a detailed account of her family's finances and it would consider giving her a loan if necessary. Her teachers told me that usually colleges look at extracurricular involvement at the high school level, as well as good grades, when they award the Presidential Scholarships which cover all fees. "Colleges won't think that pumping gas is important even if it is to provide for the family," a Plains High administrator said. But the faculty members were supportive in their recommendations of her and explained Jackie's lack of involvement in extracurricular activities as necessitated by concern for her family's circumstances. She did not get the Presidential Scholarship. Thus, in one way, her focus on education and little else at school undermined the very goals she had in getting an education.

When asked by the college to indicate the areas of study that she found most interesting, Jackie wrote in her letter of application:

> English literature is the area of study that definitely intrigues me the most. I think part of the reason is because I myself am a writer. I have always been able to see the deeper levels in literature I have read. I like the fact that literature allows a person to use his/her background and unique experiences to gain an understanding about the world the author has created. I love exploring my own intellect and the author's as well.

Her love of literature, begun as a child, was nurtured and encouraged by her English teachers. She spoke of an English teacher who told her that her poetry was gifted; this praise was a turning point for her. She wrote, "Since that afternoon my confidence in my writing has risen and I have become more emotionally stable because I have a tension reliever that allows me to deal with my problems in a constructive way." She saw her most significant out-of-class achievement as receiving awards for some of her poems and short stories and having one of her poems published. Her real love was literature. "It is always fun to get into a book and forget about the rest of the world," she said. Literature was the pivotal point of contact between Jackie and the school.

Jackie's main outlet for her passion was her poetry. She wrote passionately. Several teachers noted that much teenage poetry is angry whereas hers was insightful and controlled. Her teachers thought that her insight into people's behavior was beyond that which is normal for her age. Jackie said:

> When I'm walking down the hall, I try to notice—not necessarily the person, but the type of day it is. What does the sun look like on the ground? How is the wind blowing? How's the atmosphere in the building? things like that. I'll think about that, and then I'll notice a certain person, maybe they did something to me, and I'll put that in a poem. So it is not just the people that I notice, it is everything. . . . It's a good way to get out emotions that you necessarily can't deal with. I think I'm lucky that I can put it down.

"She is an enigma, a contradiction; she just doesn't fit the categories that you would normally associate with successful girls," another teacher commented. Comparing her with intelligent girls who did not perform well, this teacher, a male science teacher, said:

> I see Jackie as much more focused and serious and in many ways more candid. She is honest and up-front with herself and others. Sometimes she doesn't have high enough aspirations. Or perhaps it is that she doesn't let her hopes get too high. If she ever turned it all on and let herself go, I see her as having great academic abilities. I think this child can really flower, blossom. But she is afraid of something, too. Maybe it is a fear of failure of getting her hopes up and having them dashed.

In her diary, she wrote:

> The only big decision I made in life was to go to the private college where my mother went. In some ways I don't consider it a decision because it has always been my dream. I saw what that decision was doing to my parents, and, at first, I didn't let that bother me. Only recently the financial situation has cleared my head so that reality could settle in. That's when I had to decide where my priority lies, which is with my family. And this I do not even hesitate to say, all my loyalty and all my devotion belongs to my family. My future is for my parents more than for me. I know that some people think it is wrong to be that way, but I couldn't be any other way. So, my decision to continue the process for admission to the state university was easy. It was sad to let go of my dream, but I don't regret it and I'm not bitter about it. C'est la vie!

The choices Jackie made about her family and college caused her considerable stress. She was depressed and often slouched her way along the hallways of the school. But she adjusted to the limits of her choices by not compromising what was really important to her: her family and its welfare.

End Thoughts

The protective factors that assisted Jackie in becoming a successful student were found within her stressed family and within the school, among teachers who cut her some slack and in the advanced-level courses, which gave her an opportunity to express her talents as a writer. In her senior year, she used her credit with her teachers to take off more full days than any other young woman in this study—forty-four full days and and additional fifteen partial—without negative repercussions.

The value she placed on education came from her home, through the influence of her mother, who believed strongly that education is a way to overcome the limitations of social class (Connell et al. 1982). Jackie herself believed that she wanted to do better than her cousins, and the only way she could "beat" them was through education. In many ways, Jackie imitated her mother. Werner and Smith's (1982) belief that a supportive environment during infancy gives children a confidence and a coherence that account for resilience in later life seems true in Jackie's case.

The support she received from teachers, both emotional and educational (Frame 1982), upholds McCaslin and Good's (1992) point that structural support can make all the difference in enabling students with potential to make educational progress.

There was a connection between Jackie's understandings of success and her methods of achieving it—a strange contradictory mix of independent action and dependency. The meaning she gave to success was "learning more and feeling good about it. And having the teachers positive toward you." Her focus was on the future and the freedom she sought in going to a private college, a place removed from her family (Benard 1992; Cameron-Bandler 1986). While this vision for the future kept her motivated during her studies, it was not realized.

It is strange, but the very factors that supported Jackie were those that, at the same time, put boundaries and limitations on her success. Her mother's illness kept her away from school for extended periods of time. During this time, however, she engaged in intellectual discussions and read, activities that enabled her to write well and comprehend issues at a level beyond that of most other high school students. Her long hours at the gas station left her little time for extracurricular activities, which were highly regarded by the school and by the prestigious college she aspired to attend. In fact, after completing high school, she enrolled in a liberal arts course at the local state university but withdrew during her sophomore year to take up full-time employment, "to support her family."

Chapter 4

Alexis: I Need to Achieve

Alexis is a tall, thin African American woman who graduated from Plains High in 1992 with the highest GPA (3.9) of the sixteen African American girls in the senior class. Alexis was an outstanding and successful student in many ways, and her vibrant personality, and leadership qualities helped give her a prominent public image. Her activities revolved around the presentation of herself as a "leader" of the other African American students, a situation most of the black students were wise to. An intelligent girl with a great deal of insecurity, Alexis put her energy into high-profile extracurricular activities rather than classwork. Yet Alexis resisted, more than any of the other girls in the study, being singled out as a successful student.

During her senior year at school, Alexis was captain of the cheerleaders and their choreographer; president of the African American Club; the only African American member of Interact, the prestigious service organization whose members are nominated by teachers; a member of Speech Club, which won several state awards that year; a member of school choir; and a member of the Principal Scholars Program for academically talented African American students. At the 1992 Awards Night, she won four awards: one of the three Urban League Scholarships presented to African American students; the Alpha Kappa Alpha Sorority Scholarship; the Martin Luther King Scholarship Award for contributions to civil rights and human relations; and a Speech Club Varsity Award. She was accepted into a large state university to study business. Like many students today who try to improve their scores on standardized tests, she took the ACT three times in 1991 and on her last round scored 19 in English, 27 in math, and 18 in reading. Despite these achievements, the outward mask of success covered a troubled and often deeply distressed young woman.

Alexis's Biography

Alexis was born and raised in central Illinois and moved from time to time between two towns, one where her great-grandmother lived and the other where her parents lived. She said that her family—mom, dad, and older sister—lived in "the projects" (low-income housing) until she was two or three; then they moved to a house. Her aunts, uncles, and cousins visited frequently, and she often stayed over at their homes. Alexis said little about her family, especially her early childhood years.

Her family lived in a middle-class area where the lawns were neatly manicured and all the houses were large. Her home had the layout and usual trappings of a middle-class family—china cabinets with glassware, dining room table separated from the kitchen area, living room, a large family area with a huge TV set, and bedrooms upstairs. Alexis reported that her family was financially secure—she was unable to qualify for financial aid to attend college because her parents' income was too high. Her parents bought her a computer but no software, so it was inoperable. She typed her assignments on the school's computers.

Alexis's mother worked as a clerk at a large institution in town; she never went to college. Alexis spoke of her mother with ambivalence. On the one hand, she was troubled by her drinking and her continual fighting with her father. She believed that her parents' problems were often taken out on her. "When she is yelling at me, I just sit there. If I say anything, she says, 'Shut up or I'll slap you.'" On the other hand, Alexis admitted that her mother placed a high priority on education and, when she brought home a bad report card, punished her by depriving her of her car or forbidding her to visit her friends. She said, "Mom is something else; she is filled with common sense at times."

Her mother's political views influenced her greatly. She had a strong sense of African American history and classified herself as a militant black woman. Alexis was proud of this. She thought that part of her mother's problem was that her father was continually "downing" her. "He expected her to be like those young girls on those porno movies. It just gets me down listening to them fight all the time."

Her father was a blue-collar worker in town. He had obtained an associate degree from a junior college. It was with her father's mother, brothers, and sisters that Alexis liked to relax and spend her out-of-school time. She was close to her aunts and uncles in age too. They lived in the poorer end of town, and it was there that Alexis obtained her knowledge of what it is like living in poverty, with illegal drugs and, recently, with several violent deaths as part of the landscape.

Her sister was four years older than Alexis and lived in another state with her boyfriend. Alexis thought that her sister was closer to her mother's side of the family, whereas she was closer to her dad's side. Her sister, she said, gave her family a lot of grief. She had dropped out of college and was always asking her parents for money. Alexis did not want to end up like her sister; she saw her as a failure, although she admired her for keeping a job that enabled her to buy a car and furniture. After spending part of the summer holidays visiting with her sister, Alexis came to admire the way she had made a life for herself on her own. During the summer, Alexis also found out that she and her sister had different fathers. This discovery, she thought, helped her understand inconsistencies in the way her father treated the two of them. She had always thought that he favored her.

During her final year of school, Alexis felt some pressure to engage in sexual relations and discussed this with her closest confidants. They encouraged her to maintain her virginity. In her words:

> I don't have sex. I abstain. Some people don't believe me when I tell them that I'm a virgin, but I am because I haven't found the right person yet and because I am frightened of the diseases. A lot of college boys think high school girls are easy. I get my support from my two friends. One time when I was thinking about having sex just to see what it was like, Tonisha said to me, "It's OK to be a virgin." I liked that, and it helped me to stay the way I am.

Alexis said that sex education in schools gave the impression that it is OK to engage in sexual relations as long as you use protection. But she thought this attitude just lowered women's status.

At the beginning of her senior year, Alexis found the tensions of home life, a job, and schoolwork too much. She wrote a long suicide note that she intended to send to her sister but instead left it at school, where a teacher found it. It was passed on to the school social worker, who traced the unsigned letter to Alexis. "It was my cry for help," she told the social worker.

The school notified her parents and they responded with anger. More arguments followed, and Alexis ran away from home. The social worker suggested that the family get counseling, which they did, but not for long. Alexis's parents did not know that for well over a year before this event, counselors at school had been trying to help Alexis with her family situation. She had not told her parents because her mother believed that "people should solve their own problems." The school counselors became her "moms away from home," and she frequently stayed with them when she couldn't take the pressure in her own home anymore.

In the last six months of 1992, there were six homicides in the town, all of the victims known to Alexis. In our last interview, she stared at me and said, "It is just hard to believe that these people are finished. I just want to get in there and tell them to stop. After I get my degree, I want to come back and work for my people." All these murders affected her deeply, especially the death of her uncle. He was murdered the morning of the senior prom, shot in retaliation for raping a woman. He was twenty-three years old, had five children by three women, and had just been released from jail on probation. In her diary, Alexis later wrote: "I find myself missing my uncle Zapa. I betcha he would listen to me. I'll admit he was never on top of my list, but I felt he was gonna change. Why did he have to die? It was too soon for Zapa to die. Just too soon."

The night of the senior prom, Alexis dressed in a black gown. She looked stunning, but her shoulders were hunched, and there was sadness in her eyes. She did not engage in much conversation, nor did she dance with her partner, a boy about two years her junior. She did not dance with anyone.

Alexis planned to get a masters degree and a doctorate in business. "My ambition is to want. You have to have a case of the wants. That's what Melva Kelly said when she came to talk with the African American students as a guest speaker, and I haven't forgotten that," Alexis explained. What made Alexis a successful student was her longing for things to be different and the attention and praise she received from her teachers, who provided her with many opportunities to engage and display her talents.

Alexis was well-known at school, and very aware of her desire for popularity. Her teachers sometimes found her unable to make unpopular decisions because she didn't want to lose her status. She swung from being very vibrant and full of energy and able to carry an enormous workload to being severely depressed and unable to cope. One day she fainted as a result of sheer exhaustion.

Alexis's Schooling

Alexis's weeks were like a roller-coaster ride: emotional highs one day, a deep depression the next. On a good day, one would hear these comments from Alexis:

- Be the best you can.
- Instill education into kids.
- I just love school.
- There is pleasure in knowing things about yourself and others.
- Getting to know different cultures makes you more open-minded about people.
- I'm noticed here.
- I can't understand why people don't like school.
- We have committed and dedicated students here.
- It turns me on when kids are committed.
- I've grown so much this year and learned so much about myself.
- Leadership gives you strength.
- I get a high when kids say to me "you are going to go far."
- If kids have high expectations of me then I have to live up to that.

And on days when everything was bad, you heard:

- I hate that class.
- I can't stand teachers that don't teach.
- I don't like freshman girls—too many of them have the attitude.
- I've been having a bad week, and this is only Tuesday.
- My birthday was boring.
- I hate attitudes.
- College has got to be better than high school.
- It's crazy; I'm just all by my little self.
- I have funeral sickness—too many deaths.

In her last semester, Alexis chose four out of six classes that were extremely boring in content and chaotic in procedure. By the end of each day, she was emotionally down.

During the first period, Alexis was a TA for an African American teacher who had taught at Plains High for more than twenty years and was one of Alexis's supporters. This teacher spoke of her affectionately:

Even though Alexis says that I am one of the people who knows her, I was thinking that I really don't know her at all. I find her a very likable, warm person. She is reliable and trustworthy, and when I assign her something to do, she does it. Sometimes I see her sad. But I think things don't go right at

home, and she gets grounded for something. But she is responsible, outgoing, self-motivated, and seems to be determined to make it one way or another. She is a fun-loving kid and I don't think she has to study that much.
She's not a five-point-oh student but feels that she can get a passing grade
without having to study a lot. . . . I expect a lot from her, and even though
we are not in class together, I think that I've communicated that to her.

Alexis said that this teacher was like a mom to her. She thought that
the teacher was "in her face" so that she would do well, and she appreciated that.

Alexis was the captain of the cheerleaders. This was an activity in
which she could show and share her talents as a leader and as a choreographer. The PE teacher explained how a captain is selected and
how Alexis became the group's captain: "She was just way off the
scale in leadership." But over the year, she saw Alexis come to class
depressed a lot. She said, "They all have bad days, but there was a
period of about two months when she came in depressed all the time."
This was the time when she was often staying away from her parents.

Alexis's history teacher said:

When Alexis gets depressed, she says she doesn't want to live anymore, she
doesn't want to go on. If she is depressed, she won't want to practice or do
anything positive; it is very, very apparent. If she is in a good mood, she'll
come in bouncy, vivacious, and full of energy. Alexis is also a people pleaser.
She doesn't like to displease anyone. There is a lot of insecurity in her. She's
scared of hurting people, and I think she is scared of rejection. She doesn't
want people not to like her. That fear of rejection has also helped her to be
successful. She is an overachiever, too.

Alexis received many hours of counseling at school that were meant
to help her cope with her personal problems. These sessions often
took place during class time, a fact that did not seem to worry the
teachers. Her classes were often boring and tedious. The following
extracts from my field notes highlight the tedium and show that Alexis
found meaning and success in extracurricular activities.

A Day in Alexis's Life at School

In the business class, the blinds are drawn, and the sunlight filters between
the blind and the window. The lights are on. The chairs squeak as students
rock back and forth on them. Alexis does her homework for English under
the desk. The teacher has a class of 25, with twice as many boys as girls. The

teacher opens his book and asks the class a definition. No one knows the answer, or the students are not saying. After quizzing several students, he gives up and tells them the answer. He tells the class to open the book to another page and asks simple questions on a table of information in the text. The students answer incorrectly and confuse him. Next he assigns every student a different question to answer on his or her own. A student yells from the back of the class that he has nothing to write with. Another student throws a pen across the room. While the pen is in midair, the teacher calls out, "Don't throw that." The student who catches the pen falls off his chair and lands heavily on the floor. The class laughs. The teacher walks over to him and tells him to get up, then turns and says to the boy who threw the pen, "You have a 35-minute detention." Alexis begins to argue with the teacher that this is unfair. The detention remains. As the class settles back into answering their individual questions, the teacher moves around, asking the students the answers. I asked Alexis why she took this class. "It's a sort-of blow-off class. I didn't want anything too hard. But I hate it."

The next class, French, also has drawn blinds, lights on. The students sit passively as the teacher asks questions and they answer. I find myself biting my finger to keep awake. Fifty minutes later we eat lunch in the cafeteria. Here the majority of the students are African American. They sit in their groups and talk. Alexis sits with her friends, and they gossip about who is going with whom and what they are going to do on the weekend. Alexis has her English homework on the lunch table and makes half-hearted attempts to do it. On the way out, one of the lunch supervisors draws me aside and tells me that he taught some of the students I was sitting with in their freshman year. I ask him what they were like as students. He tells me that "Alexis was emotionally distant, and it seemed like she had a chip on her shoulder." He expressed some concern that I would be spending my time with students whom he perceived as not successful.

After lunch, we move on to math. Alexis complains that math is what brings her GPA down. The teacher gives students problems to do and hands them an answer sheet. In this class, Alexis does her English homework for the next period.

As I walk into the English classroom, I see a sign which reads, WHEN YOU FIND YOURSELF ARGUING WITH A COMPLETE FOOL, MAKE SURE THAT HE'S NOT DOING THE SAME THING. Next to the sign are pinned the rank-in-class sheets, which list the students according to their scores. Alexis is the only African American student in this class of 29. The teacher is well prepared; she outlines the assessment requirements and answers the students' questions. She delays only briefly on distractions and returns to the topic of the day. Alexis listens quietly and asks questions when needing clarification of what to do.

As soon as the tone sounds signaling the end of the 50 minute period, the students immediately rise and move out into the hallway to their lockers. Being in middle or advanced programs for some subjects, Alexis is not in the same classes as her African American friends, and so the hallways are the times for greetings and gossip.

During the last class of the day, choir, Alexis sits at the back of the room; her face looks drawn and tired. She seems to have hit an emotional low. The class is disruptive and chatty. A girl walks in late and is told to get rid of her gum. The girl goes over to the trash can and pretends to spit. The teacher revises previous work and certain parts of it that the students don't know. She smiles and doesn't seem perturbed by the disruption in the class. Alexis tells me that she usually skips this class (but I note that on her final report she gets an A).

At the end of the day, Alexis goes to the cafeteria to continue training the new students for next year's cheerleader tryouts. Her day has been fairly uneventful. After school, she often has other meetings to go to, a speech competition to practice for, or 101 other things which draw her into the school and its activities. It is at these extracurricular events that she finds her teacher support and the meaning that holds her fragile and disrupted life together (Field notes).

Alexis's Relationships with Her Teachers

Alexis's earliest memories of school were of being bussed to school in the third grade. She spoke about being picked out as a student with potential:

The kids hated me. I tried to get along with them, but then I realized they don't need me. Anyway, they are not going anywhere now. My mom says I was a perceptive little kid. I ran away once on my tricycle with an empty brown-paper bag. I liked elementary school, and in grade five I had a black teacher who paid a lot of attention to me.

"Why did she pay a lot of attention to you?"

"I guess because I had a lot of potential. I was in school not just to joke and play around. I wanted to do something with my life and not be in the ghetto all my life."

"How did she judge you as a person with potential?"

"I think teachers know just by watching a student—if they do their homework and are not fighting. Basically, they know who wants to be in school and who doesn't. Those who have been in the profession a long time can pick out those students."

Alexis spoke of an elementary school teacher who knew a great deal about black history, and this impressed her. But what inspired her to learn the most were teachers with "energy." They were the ones who "wanted you to learn, and made you want to learn." In high school, Alexis had the affection and attention of the five African American teachers and several others as well. She said, "What's been good for me? Well, teachers' care. I'm noticed around here basically by most teachers and administrators. I don't know how that came to be."

Alexis was a leader. She was visible as president of the African American Club, captain of the cheerleaders, and a spokesperson for African American students. She was chosen to introduce the Reverend Jesse Jackson Jr. at a school assembly when he visited Plains High. She eagerly sought these leadership opportunities, and they were offered by teachers who saw her potential. She also solicited comfort and direction from the African American faculty members who gave her their support. "All my moms at school," she called them. These teachers "get on my case from time to time," she said—and appreciated.

But Alexis lamented the fact that there were not many African American teachers. There were 5 out of a faculty of 114: two in PE (male), one in business (male), two in counseling (female), and only one in an academic subject (female). When the end-of-the-year staff cuts were announced, the African American history teacher was the first to go; she had been at the school for two years. Alexis was visibly upset when she found out that this teacher would be leaving:

> We need an African American teacher who knows something about our history. They [all students] need to know about our history so that in the end they would say, "I know why African Americans act the way they do." That would stop a lot of the racial slurs and tensions if we knew about each other's history. We learn about Martin Luther King, but he was not the only one in the civil rights movement. What about Rosa Parks?

Alexis made a link between effective teaching of African American history and the presence of an African American faculty. The same link was made by an African American teacher:

> One of the reasons black students don't do well is that they have no black teachers. A lot of the black kids are not middle class; they are poor. Poor people often don't know how to help themselves, and so they need twice the reinforcement that white students do. When they do not receive that, the lag is great.

In the classes I attended with Alexis, I did not see very much criticism of her work. In fact, she was always praised, and one teacher, when asked to comment on Alexis's abilities said, "She is not a disruptive student!"

Alexis's essays were often on black issues and contained unreferenced statements and generalized, repetitive rhetoric similar in style to political speeches. Her own speech-making style was the same. She said that she was never very good at English and confessed that she read very little. While allowing students the freedom to express themselves is important, the lack of direction and the lack of constructive comments on Alexis's work did leave one wondering why this was so when other students, like Jackie, received detailed critical analysis of their written work. Was the unqualified acceptance of her writing and her rhetoric a form of racism? In her final year at school, Alexis received a D in Literature; Jackie, an A.

Alexis's Display of Leadership

Alexis was a people pleaser; she longed for close relationships and friendship. But she was never satisfied with the relationships she had. Her friends often referred to the fact that Alexis was somewhat distant in her relationships. One of her girlfriends said:

> I think Alexis is a really goofy, really sweet girl. I don't know how to express my feelings toward her. I wish she wouldn't get into the kinds of things she gets into sometimes [like sorting out other students disagreements and relationships] because she is not tough enough. When things happen, she hurts really easily. She is sweet, and she wants everyone to like her. We talk about it sometimes, but even if you are a friend, you don't want to tell people too much. They have to find out for themselves.

While Alexis wanted people to like her, she kept an emotional distance. This caused her grief and made her lonely, too. Because she lived in a predominantly white middle-class area of town, she tried to make friends with African American students who lived in the poorer end of town. She didn't want to be seen as a "sellout," a term used by African Americans for those who dissociate themselves from other members of their race. Toward the end of 1992, an incident at Plains High showed some of the tensions that were generated by the sellout issue.

Lists were drawn up by unknown girls and circulated among the African American students. There were lists of "ugly guys," "cute guys," "whores," "dogs," "girls who think they are all that," and "the sellouts." The list that caused the most controversy was the sellout list. Alexis was not on this sellout list but was seventh on the list of "girls who think that they are all that."

At first, students took it as a joke and began calling one another by their list number and name: "Number seven girl who thinks she is all that!" Alexis said that this was the best way to counteract the intentions of those who wrote the lists and to diffuse an angry situation. She explained "Some of us made up a new list, 'girls who *know* they are all that!' We are giving them the reaction they don't want."

One of the administrators was upset by the attitude that any academically successful African American student was a sellout and asked Alexis to call a meeting to discuss the issue in an open forum. Alexis responded, "I thought, yes, let's make this even more positive, and let's get all the sellouts and the girls who think they are all that and see what they have to say. It is going to be hot!"

About sixty students turned up for the meeting. Alexis stood at the front. She had asked some African American university students to attend and hoped they would provide some perspective on "dogging" (treating one another with disrespect, trying to bring one another down). She opened the meeting by noting the issue of the lists and asked students to comment on them. Alexis guided the responses so that different groups of students had their turns to talk. The main point of contention was whether African American students could have white friends or mix with whites and not be called sellouts. Views from both sides were given by those present. The meeting was rowdy, and students seemed uninhibited by the fact that several counselors and teachers were present.

The meeting did not seem to move toward a resolution, but at the end Alexis was obviously very pleased with herself and felt that the airing of views was beneficial in itself. She said that this meeting was one of the highlights of her achievements at school. Of the adults at the meeting, some thought it a waste of time while others thought it beneficial to allow the students the opportunity, and a forum in which to air such views. One senior African American staff member was worried that the meeting might get out of control, and she was pleased that it ended without incident. The forum seemed to take the heat out of the issue, and from that time onward less attention was given to the lists.

Fordham and Ogbu (1986) suggested that when black students strove for and achieved success, they were often regarded by their peers as having accepted mainstream "white" values and as having rejected cultural solidarity with their "home" ethnic groups. Fordham (1988) said that black students, in striving for success, found conflict between the individualistic, competitive nature of American education and the black fictive kinship system. Students overcame this dilemma, she suggested, by developing a raceless strategy while in school. This was not the case for Alexis, however, for she proudly claimed her blackness and saw her success at school in terms of her leadership of the black students.

For all Alexis's leadership in school, she craved the support for herself that she so frequently offered her peers. Being a peer counselor made her realize that she was not the only one with problems. Although she spoke about being lonely and needing a peer to talk to about her problems, she did speak of her close girlfriends with affection. Yet teachers noted that she seemed isolated by the very successful image that she projected. Her female PE teacher:

> Alexis is good at supporting other people, but there is something interesting about her. The girls like to be around her, but they don't support her. Her birthday was last week, and a card was passed around for everyone to sign. One girl signed it and then handed it to her. The others said, "Oh, I forgot." And this is the way it is with Alexis. There is not a real commitment to her. I would define it as jealousy because she is really successful.

When encouragement and praise came from other students, it helped Alexis achieve. After she gave the speech welcoming Jesse Jackson Jr. several students came up to her and said, "I'm so proud of you; I want to be like you." This excited her: "I have to live up to that when kids have high expectations of me. It's a pressure, but that's OK."

Alexis under Stress

Plains High had a talent show sponsored by the African American Club. It had begun several years before when the African American students believed that they were being excluded from the school-sponsored talent show because they liked different forms of entertainment—rap and soul music, and fashion shows, for example. The other talent show emphasized artistic accomplishments, comedy, instrumental music, singing, and group performances. Alexis was the student organizer of the African American Talent Show. With the support of two African American teachers and the members of the club, a group of black students put on a performance that drew more than five hundred parents and friends. From my field notes: "This was a night of vibrancy and energy. These young people have a lot of talent and skill. But only five teachers were present to see this performance. . . . A few days later there is no mention of the show."

In a nearby high school the African American Talent Show was canceled because of the fear that it would be disrupted by gangs. The principal of Plains High permitted students to go ahead but requested police security and hired security guards. "There were no problems, and the kids had a great time," stated a black counselor.

Alexis encouraged participation by non-African American students because, she said, "It is an African American-sponsored show, not an African American show." Several white students tried out and participated.

Teachers and her friends drove her around town to get the clothes required for the fashion show. A lot of time and energy was spent preparing. The African American history teacher, who was also involved in the show, said:

> Alexis has a leadership role. But she takes on so much she is pulled in twenty-five directions. She gets lots of strokes for successful things that she does, and that helps. But it doesn't get to the core of what she really needs. She uses excessive activity as a way of diverting, or not dealing with, her problems. It's a kind of frenetic activity—on the go, busy, busy, busy, not sitting and taking time to deal with emotions. If you sit and listen to her day, especially when she was preparing for the talent show, she would go home for forty minutes and supposedly she was going to eat, shower, do homework, and be back here until ten in the evening for rehearsals! She had the whole production of it, delegating responsibility, asking other people's assistance, and at the same time trying to maintain top grades in her classes. Well, her work is going to suffer. But she expects too much from herself.

During the year, Alexis took part in two educational support groups run by the school social worker. One was for African American students under stress and the other for students with "dysfunctional families." A counselor explained:

> We identify students, through different means, who are having some upheaval in their families, and we meet once a week for eight to ten weeks. We rotate periods so they don't miss the same class. It is run like a class; we have information packets for them. They do not divulge a lot of their personal information; instead, we concentrate on personal skills, problem solving, looking at roles they might play in their families, and things like that.

Participating in these groups helped Alexis. She said:

I've learned a lot about myself this year. I've grown a lot. The counselor ran some of those groups, and I was in two of them: one on families and the other one I put myself into—the one on being African American. They are kids like me who talk about their problems and get coping strategies. You realize that you are not alone. The media gives such negative images of African Americans, and I've learned something about that.

End Thoughts

For Alexis, success was in the recognition given her for making public the issues of the school's African American students. She wanted African Americans to have a greater say in the school and through her own reputation was able to give impetus to that cause. Alexis adopted the "speaking out" strategy identified by Cohen (1996) and discussed extensively by hooks (1989). She was noticed because of her public activities and used this credit to defend students when they were in trouble as well as to promote recognition of African American students and their needs. She advised other students to "get your homework done, and don't fight" as a recipe for success.

Alexis was the first to take a stand against perceived injustices, however, and, like her mother, was an activist. Unlike Fordham and Ogbu's (1986) students, who used a "raceless strategy" to become successful at school, Alexis used her very identification as an African American student leader to bring her success and recognition. She secured approval from teachers and counselors (Davies 1983; Kerr 1985; Weis 1985a), although not all her teachers were convinced of her success.

Alexis had several of the key factors that Kerr (1985) found in the backgrounds of the successful women she studied: a mission in life, guidance and encouragement during adolescence, a refusal to accept the limitations of gender, and an ability to combine roles.

The protective factors that enabled Alexis to become a successful student were found within the school. The teachers who gave her the greatest support were the African Americans. But they were few in number, and as Foster (1993) pointed out, "Rarely have African American teachers fared well in unitary school systems" (286).

Alexis sought opportunities to present herself in public, and she was given such opportunities by the school. She participated in speech competitions; she introduced public figures at school assemblies; she gained the attention of members of the administration and the teachers. They expected her to do well, even to the point of overlooking her performance in academics. Interestingly, Alexis was touted as an academically successful student, but the criteria for judging this were not so much her grades as her presence.

Chapter 5

Sabrina:
Life Is Like an Endless Battle

Sabrina, a special-education student since middle school, was a member of the National Honor Society and one of the first young women recommended to this study as a successful student. A special-education teacher said, "Sabrina's deficit areas which make her eligible for learning-disabilities services are written expression, applying phonic skills in reading, difficulty with long- and short-term memory and auditory retrieval. She is in the average range intellectually (IQ of 96)."

Despite her disabilities, she worked "extremely hard" and graduated from high school midyear with a GPA of 4.6. She was included as part of this study of success in school because more than ten percent of the students at Plains High received some form of assistance from the special-education department. What the faculty of that department regarded as a success story is important in the context of a study of success at Plains High.

Sabrina was a tall, well-built young woman with a round, fair face. She worried constantly about her weight. In class, she was quiet and worked all the time. She listened intently and worked on whatever task was assigned. She rarely initiated discussion but questioned a teacher when she didn't understand what was to be done. According to the business teacher, Sabrina was one of the most successful students in the Office Occupations Work Program, in which students were released from school in the afternoon to go to work and for which they received school credit. She was reliable and hardworking at work just as she was at school. In contrast to her successes at school, however, her home life presented a picture of chaos, conflict, and stress.

Sabrina's Biography

Sabrina had an older sister as well as a half brother and a half sister from her mother's previous marriage. Although both her parents graduated from high school, none of her siblings did. Both her sisters left school pregnant, a point she emphasized with strong disapproval. One sister had run away from home when she became pregnant. Her brother had been jailed for some time, then spent six months in a hospital recovering from alcoholism. She said her mother drank every day and came home drunk late at night. When Sabrina was young, her father would say to her, "You can't have friends stay over; you wouldn't want them to see your mother like that, would you?"

In the year that I spent with Sabrina, I never heard her say a good word about her mother. There were few indications that there were many good words to be said for her. She beat her daughter when she was drunk, didn't visit her when she spent some time in the hospital, and refused to pay the bills when she was discharged. The only time she came to Plains High during Sabrina's three and a half years there was for her induction into the National Honor Society. Sabrina constantly made some complaint about her parents, particularly her mother. The complaints ranged from dislike of their surveillance of her activities—she said they watched her closely because her sisters had been in so much trouble—to her saying that she had never really had a mother.

In her junior year in high school, she was ill and said she was in a lot of pain most of the time, a fact her teachers confirmed. Sabrina said she thought that being in pain was how most people were. She gradually became overweight, and each time she went to the doctor, she was given a pregnancy test. When Sabrina said that she couldn't be pregnant, she was told, "That's what all the girls say, darling!" The kids at school teased her about being fat, too.

Some of her teachers were well aware of her weight gain and problems at home and knew how hard she worked despite these setbacks. One of her more supportive teachers said:

> When I met Sabrina in her freshman year, she was fat, lots of pimples, her skin tone was sick, and she was physically unattractive. The doctors kept giving her pregnancy tests until they did an exam and discovered the tumors. They wanted to leave the operation for a while, but Sabrina insisted that she have it. They removed two five-pound tumors. She lost weight rapidly and told me that it was wonderful to be out of pain. She has a lot of determination which carries her through. If she doesn't understand something, she comes to me for help before or after school. I think she is more mature than other kids. She just knocks herself out working.

Sabrina was angry about the fact that the doctors thought she was pregnant and the fact that her mother did not visit her. She stated:

> My mother didn't come to visit me while I was in the hospital because she was too busy with her boyfriends. I don't know why my dad puts up with her. My mother is going on fifty, and she is like a teenager. She's had two husbands and four children and about ten boyfriends. She doesn't know what she wants in life.

Sabrina did not want me to meet with her parents because, she said, "They are crazy. They put on a false face for visitors." I asked several times to meet with them because I wanted to hear the story of their daughter's school success from their perspective. Each time I asked, however, Sabrina insisted that I not meet them, and I believed that this insistence should be respected. Her story is constructed from observations and from interviews conducted with her and her teachers and friends.

When I first met Sabrina, she was living in a trailer home with her brother, his wife, and their two children. She said that she had left home because she would not take her mother's abuse anymore. Several teachers told me that they believed she was an abused child. At this time, she was holding down four jobs because her brother made her pay half the rent and provide food for all of them. She said that some nights she got only about three hours' sleep. She often appeared stressed during interviews, and sometimes she cried as we talked. She said, "I still get in my really depressed moods where I can't find a reason to be depressed. I'm just depressed, I guess, over the whole picture. I can't come up with just one thing that I'm depressed about."

She had talked with the school counselor only once. "I don't like complaining about my problems because there is always someone worse off than me," she said.

After she lived at her brother's trailer for about three months, her father came and loaded her things on to a truck and took her home.

Sabrina said she would like to say that her dad was one of the people she admired, but "he is weak about my mom." She said that her father had been a major support of hers throughout her life. He had bought her a car even though that caused him to go into debt. He later sold the car, and because they didn't get enough money to pay back the loan, she was paying for a car she no longer had.

Sabrina was very fond of her nieces and nephews, "although they drive me crazy." She said that she liked to take care of her brother's little daughter "because she looks like me." This baby was often in the hospital with asthma and, Sabrina said, "is supposed to be on a venti-lator, but my sister-in-law doesn't use it as often as she should."

Although her parents rarely attended functions or meetings at Plains High, her father did attend her annual Individualized Educational Pro-gram (IEP) meetings.

The teachers involved in the IEP said that they got the impression Sabrina's parents wanted her to finish school as quickly as possible and get into the workforce to earn some money. They encouraged her to graduate early, which she did, having accumulated enough credits to graduate at the end of the first semester of her senior year. After graduation, she continued to work part-time in the local bookstore where she had been employed with the Office Occupations Work Pro-gram.

A literacy specialist who had worked closely with Sabrina said she thought Sabrina's role in the family was that of a savior: "In a dysfunc-tional family, one has many roles, one of which is savior. She tries to bring positive attention to the family by covering up their dysfunction. They keep track of her because she is their savior. This is typical of Sabrina's case."

Sabrina told me that her family liked to hide things about them-selves. "I don't like to talk about my family a lot because I am embar-rassed by them," she said.

Several years before, the family, especially the mother, had gone through a religious phase. They joined a fundamentalist Christian church that required all the women to wear skirts and blouses and tie their hair back. The church was strictly against dancing and gambling, Sabrina said that her mother no longer went to the church but was still influenced by its teachings as far as behavior was concerned. She said, "My parents were more worried about the way I looked rather than how I was doing at school. They put more time into finding out ex-actly where I was instead of how my grades were doing." Sabrina was critical of her mother for the inconsistency she perceived between her behavior and that which she expected of her daughter.

In her freshman year, Sabrina wrote and illustrated her autobiogra-phy for a class assignment. It was full of photos and memorabilia of her life. In it a section entitled "We Are a Part of Every Person," she described those who gave her support:

> My dad is one of the people that keep me going. He is the best dad anybody could have. He's a very mello kind of guy. . . . My sister is more like my best friend, and my grandma has helped me to grow into the person I want to

be. . . . My uncle [a friend of the family called Uncle] taught me inconse-
quential things. Like don't get worried or upset over little things. Looks and
size don't matter, it's what's inside that counts. He also said "life is like an
endless battle, you can win it if you have the right weapons."

Sabrina did not mention her mother in the assignment work. In one
section, however, she wrote, "I have some very strong opinions about
child abuse, alchoalishen, mixed mariges, drugs, and wars. . . . Any
person to hurt a child is sick in the head."

Sabrina spoke of her grandmother with great affection. She and
her father traveled out of town to visit her at least once a month.
During the time of this study, the grandmother died, and Sabrina spent
some time grieving her loss. At the funeral, she found out that this
woman she had been calling Grandma was not her biological grandmother but the grandmother of her half siblings. She was shocked and
upset that her mother had deceived her for so long.

When asked whether she considered herself poor, average, or rich,
Sabrina said that this was a difficult question to answer because of the
way the family arranged its finances. Her mother earned her own
wage and kept it separate from the family finances, and her father
payed all the bills with help from Sabrina. "If you were to put the two
wages together, we would be OK, but because we have to live off my
dad's income, we are not that well off."

She had recently become ill again, and the doctor refused to treat
her because her parents had not paid the bill for her operation. She
asked the doctor to set up an account for her since she was now eighteen and said that she would pay any future bills herself. She said,
"This was the only way I could get to see the doctor."

At home, Sabrina had a room of her own with a desk, and a set of
1990 encyclopedias that her father had won with coupons at a gro-
cery store. "But," she said, "I don't read much because of my disability. I used to get all of my homework done in study hall. Some of the
kids liked to mess up and talk, but if I didn't understand something, I
would ask."

Sabrina's Schooling

Sabrina was the type of student who was easily overlooked. She was
quiet in class, worked hard, and was not involved in the school's extracurricular activities. When she entered junior high, Sabrina was given
special-education services. At this time, she said, her attitude toward

school changed, and she began to see her teachers as helpers. She wrote in her autobiography, "I am beginning to like school. I like people to talk and be friendly. Kids said I was brown-nosing, but I think it is better to be friends than enemies." The special-education teachers took the time to be friends with students, and her study-hall teacher offered personalized help. This teacher said that she spent a lot of time with Sabrina in her freshman year just doing her assignments with her:

> Because Sabrina had problems with reading and comprehension, she compensated by spending more time doing her assignments and asking for help. In her freshman year, she was really floundering and couldn't cope with the work. For a while, I almost did the assignments for her but gradually showed her how to look for information and do them on her own. By the end of her junior year, she was totally weaned from special-education support services.

Sabrina told me that she tested "borderline" in elementary school, so she was left in the mainstream classes until she went to middle school, where her reading and comprehension problems became more acute. She felt she was being left behind the other students. With special-education services, she enjoyed the more individualized attention of the tutorial system. She said she was unable to define her disability clearly, but she knew that she needed assistance with her work: "I don't know exactly what it is that I have. I've seen on some papers that I have dyslexia, and I have a poor memory, and I'm just slow at comprehending."

Several teachers said that when Sabrina encountered obstacles to her learning, she did something about it. In one class in which she did not like the teacher, she went to her counselors and her dean and arranged to change classes. The administration was amenable to this because, as a special-education teacher noted, "she was pleasant and generally did what she was told. And she had her way of getting around the system." In Sabrina's junior year, the counselor, in conjunction with the special-education teachers, had suggested that she try a more difficult level of English and social studies. Sabrina didn't last in these classes and was happy to return to the basic-level classes. At least there she received As and recognition for her efforts. She wanted to succeed even if it meant taking level-one classes.

About getting high grades, she said:

> I had the time and the encouragement. My sister, especially, since she didn't graduate from high school, really pushed me. She said, "Go for those good

grades, and see how well you do and how well you feel that you've done so good." I just did the best I could, and I put a lot of effort toward it, and I got what I wanted. It would have been easy to say I had a disability, but then you are not going to make it anywhere. My goal is to be as independent as possible.

In praise of her teachers, she said, "they gave me the attitude that if I am to succeed *I* have to do the work. I wasn't a perfect student, and I didn't want trouble, so I kept quiet mostly."

Sabrina was nominated for membership in Interact the prestigious service organization made up of seniors who have performed well in school and who have demonstrated good citizenship. She decided not to join:

I went along to one meeting and found out that to stay in the club, you had to do all this work. I thought, "If I am to do all that work, I want to be paid for it. I haven't got time to be doing volunteer work when I need money."

Sabrina saw volunteer work as something for those who had time and money, not for those who needed to earn money.

At the school-sponsored College Night, Sabrina spoke of her desire to go to the local junior college to study nursing. But she was hesitant about approaching the booths to get information. She found out that she would have to study for an extra year to get into the program because she didn't have the prerequisites in math and chemistry. She felt her mother was pushing her to go to college but that she didn't feel like going right then.

Sabrina was the only one of the siblings in her family to graduate from high school. She felt very proud to be wearing the cap and gown on the night of her graduation but didn't understand why she didn't get to wear the gold tassels that others who graduated with a GPA of 4.5 and above got to wear. The school secretaries explained that level-one courses were not counted in the assessment of that honor.

When asked to name the best times of her schooling, Sabrina said:

The best times . . . It's kind of hard to say because I look back at everything, and it all seems so hard. I think the best time was just graduating, being able to say that I actually did it, to have that diploma in my hand and knowing that I was able to do it through all the hard times.

For Sabrina, success was just graduating and having good grades. It didn't matter to her that the grades were earned in level-one classes. The fact of graduating didn't really relate to what might happen after she completed her schooling. She just wanted to do better than her sisters. Her best times were overshadowed by her hard times, the times when she held four jobs and was getting three hours' sleep a night, moving from home to home because she didn't want to be abused anymore, and not having enough money to pay her bills. Her motivation to succeed came from her desire to escape the situation of her parents:

> I tried to be better, I think. I don't want to be in the situation that either one of my parents are in. I don't want to do wrong things. I don't even know what the word for it is, . . . like forgetting that people are important. I don't want to be the way my mom is, and I don't want to have be a hard laborer the rest of my life. My dad works hard, and it shows. I want to do something that I enjoy, not because I have to go and make a living: I want to do it because I enjoy it. So it pushes me to say, "Hey, I don't want to be down there in that situation."

Sabrina was goaded by pressures from her brother and sisters. Her brother was bankrupt and leaning on her to pay his bills. Her mother asked her to take out loans for him because she was the one with a job. But his bills were so high she didn't feel she could put herself into debt to bail him out. The memory of her sisters' getting pregnant and dropping out of school also made a big impact on her. She said, "The way it hurt my sisters to tell my parents that they were pregnant, and the way it hurt my parents to hear it, pushed me to say, 'Hey, that's not for me, not right now.'" Talking about her strengths, Sabrina said:

> I think one of my strengths is trying to finish what I have started. I don't like to start a job and let it lay. Pretty much at work I start stuff and don't have time to finish it. I really hate to let it lie. But I'm learning that I just have to let it go until tomorrow and then finish up what I did. To finish something I've started is one of my strengths. . . . My parents told me that if I wanted money, I had to get it myself. So I see work as survival. . . . I think I jump from one emotion to another. One minute I can be extremely upset, and then five minutes later I can be as happy as can be. I just jump from one emotion to another. If someone sees me depressed in the morning, they might not see me depressed in the afternoon. I just bounce from one [emotion] to another. I don't know if that is good or bad.

About the future and what it meant for her, Sabrina said that her problems would be solved if she could only find the right man. She had had several relationships, all of which ended when she discovered the men were two-timing her. Her desire for someone to "find her" was expressed in this poem which she wrote after she had left school and was working:

My love. . . . Sometimes I feel like you're not out there.
Everyone tells me I'll find you. Do I already know you?
Will I meet you tomorrow,
Next week, next month, or next year?
When I feel I need you the most I don't have you!
I need you now, I need to be loved.
I need to have you, my special friend.
The one I don't need to explain myself to, you already know.
The one I can cry to,
And not have to worry that you'll think I'm silly.
My love . . . are you out there, please find me!

Her notion of romantic love showed her desire for acceptance and love in an idealized world beyond her experience. But her desire for love and her emotional vulnerability were masked by a resilient, hard-nosed perseverance in the face of adversity.

End Thoughts

Sabrina's definition of success was having a GPA of 4.6 achieved at the lowest academic level. In Sabrina's case, Plains High accepted this as one of the multiple pathways to success. For Sabrina, her teachers, and her family, success meant recognition of achievement, but for her, success also had other connotations: she did not want to be like her parents, her brother, or her sisters who, she said, did not value education. The school's acceptance of her definition of success aided her in gaining her prize. Sabrina achieved her educational goal the night she graduated; graduation was her success, the goal she had set herself. She did this by using the study hall, seeing her teachers as helpers (Davies 1983; McCaslin and Good 1992; Weis 1985a), asking for help, organizing herself to get good grades (it didn't matter at what level), working hard and applying determination. She made school her protection and her pathway to success.

Sabrina "did school" (Cohen 1996). Her methods required her to be passive and not create trouble. This meant that she earned good grades and was described by both teachers and peers as successful. She followed carefully the teachers' prescription for success—"ask if you need help"—and it worked. She received approval, recommendations and rewards. Sabrina hated being labeled as "a special-education student" and especially disliked its association with "being dumb." Paradoxically, even though the teachers tried to get her to take mainstream classes, she fought for the right to remain in the closely supervised study hall, where she received personalized attention. It was this individual attention that enabled her to learn how to do research and present quality assignments. It also enabled the teachers to take a close interest in her private life and monitor its effects on her schooling. By the time she reached her senior year, she was regarded as an independent learner and no longer required the services of the special-education department. The ability to be independent of the support scaffold was the reason teachers recommended Sabrina as a successful student. She was the teachers' success story.

Chapter 6

Jasmine: My Two Personalities

Jasmine entered the United States with the 1980 wave of refugees from southeast Asia. She was five years old. She came with her mother and her stepfather. They were sponsored by a Christian church based in rural Illinois. Upon arrival Jasmine was given a birth date because her mother, unfamiliar with the western calendar, didn't know the equivalent. Not long after they arrived in the United States, Jasmine's little sister was born and her mother divorced her husband. She had had other partners, and one of these had sexually abused Jasmine. At the time of this research, Jasmine's family consisted of her mother and younger sister.

When Jasmine started school in the United States, she spoke no English. She said that from the time she was four or five she lost her first language, Laotian, and began speaking Tagalog, the language of the Philippines, where the family had lived in a refugee camp. This was the language she spoke with her mother at the time of the research, at least most of the time. After arriving in the United States, she began speaking English but said that she didn't want to lose Tagalog as she'd lost her first language. She believed that studying French at school, as well as English, was helping to make up for the lost first language.

Jasmine's family was Buddhist, but after their arrival in the United States, under the auspices of their sponsors they began attending Christian services. Jasmine said, "I went to church and paid attention to Bible studies, but it hasn't affected my way of life, and my mom's beliefs in Buddhism haven't affected me either. I don't consider myself to have any religious affiliation." When some Buddhist monks came to town and held a ceremony in a house near hers, she wrote in her diary, "Mom wanted me to go to the ceremony and maybe my luck would change. That's the southeast Asian belief anyway. The monks cure all sin and bad luck but things only work if you believe in them. I don't have any religious beliefs but I went."

Jasmine's story was intertwined with reflections of what her mother told her about women's roles in southeast Asia, and her experiences in and hopes for the United States:

> Until I was five, I lived in a refugee camp in the Philippines. I used to be really sick all the time because we were really impoverished. My mom was never sent to school because she wasn't a boy in the family, and the females were less prominent. So she just worked on the farm. I would probably be lower class if I were still there because our relatives are really poor. I remember my mom telling me back in her country, girls were absolutely nothing. Every time a family was started up, that couple would always attempt to have a boy.

Jasmine remembered her first impression of the new country and its people:

> We lived in a little house next to the church. It was an all-white town, and we were the only Oriental people. We didn't have a lot of fancy clothes or anything like that so a lot of the kids teased me. I wore clothes donated by the church, and they were not in style or anything. I realized that being passive attracted mockery so I learned mildly aggressive skills to make friends and to express myself. Everything was foreign to me, and I was foreign to everyone else.

One of the family's sponsors, a teacher, gave Jasmine a lot of attention. Jasmine said she remembered the classroom as very well organized, with books and toys along the wall and desks in rows. Her mother constantly reminded her that even though things were difficult here, back in her country she would have had "the worst life."

> I wouldn't have had any schooling, and I would have been cooking and lugging things around the village. Mom told me that in the United States she wanted me to get an education. And at about grade five or six I started comparing myself to other people. It was at that time that I started to develop my priorities. And finally I told myself that I wanted to be on top. You know, I would listen to the teachers tell us stories of people on drugs and how they messed up their lives. But I felt that I had come to the United States for a purpose, and it wasn't to get messed up on drugs or anything.

Jasmine's mother, who had taught herself to read, told her two girls that to get ahead, they must do well in school (see Ogbu 1991, 1994). And that was what this remarkable young woman did. By the time she entered her senior year in high school, she was a member of the school track team and the cheerleading squad, editor-in-chief of the school newspaper, secretary of the International Club, vice president of the French Honors Society, and a member of the National Honor Society, the student council, the Building Curriculum Committee, the United Way student board, and the Senior-of-the-Month Committee. In her junior year, she received the PTA Reflections Award for outstanding written work. Her GPA was 4.67, which placed her in the top 10 percent of her class of 315. Jasmine was in her junior year during the time of the study. Jasmine also worked hard at cultivating a fashionable teenage image. She dressed and behaved like many other teens in high school. She fluctuated between wanting to be thin, being on the plump side, and not caring. Her girlfriends liked to tan their skins and they got Jasmine into "this tanning phase. We want to get sooo dark!"

Jasmine's Biography

Jasmine's mother had been in three car accidents, all of them serious. The financial strain the family experienced because of the mother's inability to work was mostly felt when Jasmine wanted to join in extracurricular activities at school but could not afford them. She was excluded from several groups because she did not have the money for the equipment or for expenses associated with their activities. Over the summer after her junior year, her mother let her work for the first time to help pay some of the family's bills.

Jasmine's bedroom was distinctively her own. It was extremely well ordered and had no bed. She slept on the living-room couch or on the double bed in her sister's room in order to have more room for bookcases and her desk. On one wall was a bench lined with files of her work going back to elementary school. Along another wall she had her computer and her desk. Above her desk was a stylized picture of the face of a woman with a tear running down her cheek. A swivel chair was placed directly in front of the desk. In a glass-doored cabinet containing folders, every piece of paper was filed and stacked neatly, perhaps modeled on the orderly kindergarten classroom she had so admired on her first day of school in the United States. She had a bookcase full of magazines given to her by a friend and a set of 1953 encyclopedias given to her by her church sponsor. Lining the top of the four walls were her many certificates. Small artifacts from Laos and the Philippines hung neatly on the wall along with photos of her friends. Nothing, it seemed, was out of place. It was here that Jasmine spent hours studying and reading. Sometimes she studied all night, sometimes for more than thirteen hours at a stretch. She had a computer that her mother had bought her, on which she did all her schoolwork—she was a perfectionist in the presentation of her work. No one else was allowed in her room, a rule her mother ignored, which Jasmine said showed a lack of respect for her privacy.

Excerpts from Jasmine's diary, kept during the second semester of this research, portray the major dilemma in her life: how to free herself of her mother's restrictions. They also show Jasmine's deep conflict with and, at the same time, her strong dependence on her mother. They are printed here at length to show the detail of her double life—at home and at school—and to show the complications and stress that result from leading such a life. Her analysis of the situation, her reaction to it, and the role of her friend show the fine line between attempting suicide and making it through:

[Friday, May 1, in large, round handwriting] It's finally Friday! I've been waiting three months for this weekend—my junior prom will be great. It took me so long to save up money for my dress. I told my mom that I'd be gone for a track meet this weekend and I'd be back Sunday.

Chuck is having a party at a hotel tonight. I don't think I'm gonna get buzzed just because I'm afraid that something might happen before the prom. I am staying with a girlfriend whose parents are going to be gone. She doesn't get off work until eight so I am going to wait for her at the mall. We'll go out with some of her friends. She says John is interested in me, but my feelings are not mutual. He seems very nice but he's in a gang called the "Dawgs." I don't want to find out if they're ruthless or not. Besides Chuck would not be happy. He's very possessive and gets jealous easily. I don't want to get too involved with relationships, but I have to keep myself from being bored with school business. It's not like I try, but I get along with guys much better than with girls. One thing bothers me is that males perceive my friendliness the wrong way. . . .

It's hard for me to concentrate on school. I've been asked to the prom both freshman and sophomore year, but have been unable to go. I can't believe how excited I am. My dress is my favorite color, red. It's long satin with lace on top. I am also looking forward to meeting my boyfriend's parents. He's never wanted to introduce anyone to his parents and that made me special.

[Sunday, May 3, in small, jagged handwriting] This is one of the worst weekends of my life. It seems like the worst thing that could've happened did happen. Everything is so unfair. While I was waiting for my friend at the mall I was accused of shoplifting by two security guards that apprehended me. I am soooo mad! Being falsely accused is one of the worst things that can happen to anyone!! I was scared to call my mom (since she thought I was out of town anyway). So I called my friend, Debbie, and stayed with her Friday night. We talked about so many things including what I was gonna do. Speaking out to defend myself to the security officers was not difficult for me at all. I remained composed and avoided panic. But when I realized that confronting my mom about the situation was inevitable, a surge of frustration, anger, and most of all—fear beset my mind. I was soooo scared to face her. To be completely honest, I'd rather be dead at the time. I had been in a similar situation before, and that made it worse. My mom and I had also just touched base with each other. Things were going soo perfect!

Sitting on the bed at Debbie's house I was completely out of touch with reality. I just wanted to leave [commit suicide]. Debbie sensed that I was contemplating something so she slept outside my room at the door to make sure I didn't hurt myself. She's so much like a mother to me. I never knew a friend who cared so much that it stunned me. I didn't sleep at all and hadn't eaten since Thursday even. I was very distressed, but I had to keep myself busy. So I dug dandelions like crazy and ended up with blisters on my hands.

Then Debbie and I went back to the store for an unsuccessful attempt to get the officers to reassess what transpired the previous night. Debbie eventually brought me home to talk to my mom. I half expected a blow to the face, but what followed was worse—the silent treatment. After Debbie left, I stayed in my room not knowing what else to say to my mom. We haven't spoken since then. At this point I've identified the perpetuating cycle: mistake; outburst of anger; emotional pain; silence; resentment; anger; more silence . . . eventually mom would come to me to discuss matters. I expected the worse with my mom and it did not come, surprisingly.

[Monday, May 4] I still haven't had any communication with my mom. We pass like strangers do on the street . . . even worse. I feel the tension as if it's vibrating between us. There's no eye contact or any acknowledgment of acquaintance.

I had my English presentation at school today. I was the interviewer and it was very difficult. Our group volunteered and got 100 percent and it surprised me. I actually had to pretend to be the broadcaster, Connie Chung. I wanted to avoid thinking about the situation I was in. I guess that's why I did so well—very ironic!

I hate my life so much. Here I am a student with potential straight As, editor-in-chief of a school publication, a leader in a dozen organizations, and I have a criminal record. It doesn't make any sense. Wednesday and Thursday will be symbolic. Wednesday I have Awards Night at which I will receive an Outstanding Journalist plaque, Quill and Scroll Society induction, and Outstanding English Award. Then Thursday I have a court hearing. I can't think of a better paradox. I'm really losing faith and interest in everything. I have an urge to quit everything and go sit in the corner of the world where I can't get myself into these situations.

[Wednesday, May 6] I haven't talked to mom yet. The intensity of pain and anger is so prevalent in the house, you can feel it the second you step foot through the door. I try not to come home until I have to. I end up going to my room anyway. I have not eaten anything for almost a week. I've had one glass of orange juice and thirteen cups of tea since I've been home Saturday morning. I'm just not hungry. I missed Awards Night and I had completely missed prom, two parties, post prom, dinner, and Chuck's seventeenth birthday. At first I acted like it didn't matter, but it did. I've wanted my mom to see me receive my awards since the first day of school. All my friends were expecting to see me there.

Mom's not going to the hearing with me tomorrow unless I ask her. She told Debbie that she didn't care what legal obligations she had to be present. If they took me away—Oh well! I figured as much. Debbie talked to me and said, "Jasmine, it's up to you to save yourself. You <u>have</u> to talk to your mom. You have no other choice if you want to stay at home." The truth was—I wish they would take me away. But I talked to Debbie and I'm sitting here on my hardwood floor next to a lit candle in the darkness in front of the mirror wondering where I'm going to start. I hate this.

[Thursday, May 7, in larger handwriting] Well, I finally had the nerve to speak up and face my mom. Wednesday night I sat down with her and talked for four hours until one-thirty A.M. I apologized, suggested solutions, told her how I felt, and asked her to go down to the Police Station for the hearing. Everything at school seemed better the next day.

It's not as bad now that my mom is behind me. We're gradually convalescing, but it will be a long time before she will trust me again. But I've made a very important decision. I am never going to lie to my mother again unless it's going to really hurt her. If I want to do something, school related or not, I'm going to ask. If she says "no," we'll discuss it. This is the way it has to be. I have to stop keeping her out of my life. That means I'll need to keep her more up-dated with school and actually let her meet my friends. I know my life will be less of a strain if I have less secrets to worry about.

[Friday, May 8, in large, well-rounded handwriting] So much has happened within the past week. I can't believe it's Friday again. Mom and I are on much better terms. She's still expecting me to be around more so I've sacrificed spending time in my room. I try to be around her as much as possible and I hope things work out.

[Saturday, May 9] When calamities penetrate your entity and leave a puncture through which hope leaks, you must seal it with dignity and allow it to solidify with time. The more I think about that the better I feel. When things happen, waiting for despair to pass, can seem endless and hopeless. Through this whole ordeal, though it hasn't ended, I've learned many things. The first of which is: Silent anger between two people bonded by love echoes farther than the angry cries of many bonded by cause. The second thing I've learned can best be put as: The past is a valuable reference source to which we must always consult in understanding the present and planning the future. To recognize happiness we must know despair. . . . The most important thing I've learned (and it sounds like a paradox) is: We must all face the truth about lies. . . . I realized that I've reached the point where my whole life is one big lie. And that statement is the only truth I know.

I hadn't changed my mind about quitting my school activities until my mom said something. Her words expressed pride in me for the great things I've accomplished. I never heard her actually say that because she assumed I knew. Those few words transformed me from a quitter into someone else. Someone who has one more person to please besides herself. Before I say to myself, "I'm going to involve myself in all of my interests—just like before," I really have to think am I really capable of handling all of these commitments? The answer is a complicated one. Yes, I am capable, but only up to a certain point. As long as my family and home-life do not become too stressful, then I can handle all of these organizations.

Well I have to clean up my room. It's never, ever been so messy before. I just completely trashed it Wednesday afternoon because I was sooo angry. That's something I've never done before, but I was too upset to count to ten . . . or even 100 for that matter!

[Sunday, May 10] Today is Mother's Day. I had no money, so I scrounged up some change and went to the store to get some flowers. I arranged a beautiful bouquet and a card and gave it to mom.

The emotional turmoil that Jasmine experienced during this incident was not isolated. She lived with such tension most of her life. Ogbu (1994) said that the difference between success and failure among cultural minorities is the cultural knowledge and strategies students bring with them from their communities. The intensity with which Jasmine lived out her life could be seen in the way she applied herself to her academic life.

Jasmine's Schooling

Jasmine's opportunities for involvement at school were abundant. She wanted to be in as many leadership positions as possible. Hence, she volunteered for nearly every position that presented itself. There were no limits to the number of clubs a student could join, and sometimes Jasmine thought she had taken on too much. She was regularly elected director of a play or leader of a group discussion or head of a debate. One teacher noted:

Jasmine really wants to do well, but I have concerns about the way she works with others. She was elected as leader of the play for this semester, and that is a tribute to her. She is a strong student. But even when we have group quizzes, she takes too much control. She doesn't delegate much. Her tendency is when we do a quiz, she'd be reading the questions by herself and answering them by herself. So I would point out that they weren't functioning as a group. She is a bit inconsiderate about how others feel, too.

She preferred doing the job for them rather than having them do it in a way that was different from the way she wanted it done. This caused conflict when students thought she was taking over. Students both loved and hated her for this style of leadership.

"Jasmine is an exceptional girl who has such high standards and expects everybody else to be the same," said the dean of students. Jasmine complained that she hated group work because when quizzes were done in a group, she often got more wrong than when she did them on her own. She was very much oriented toward performance. The tension between what the teachers saw as a good learning strategy and what Jasmine thought is captured in these comments:

[Teacher] In high school, kids are not used to learning cooperatively. They say they hate group work because they have a typical Jasmine situation: she does all the work, and the others freeload. But she is gradually learning to work cooperatively and not allowing those freeloader situations to exist.

[Jasmine] It's not my fault that they put committed students with those who don't care less about their work. At the beginning of the year, that is how the teachers organized the group: those who liked work were put with the loafers. At the end of the year, after I spoke to the teacher, he changed things around and put the workers together and the loafers together. This was good because we worked hard together, and because the loafers didn't have anyone to do the work for them, they had to do some work themselves.

She found the classes that used cooperative learning very difficult because she was forced to listen to others and be guided by their suggestions. Occasionally she found herself in a situation where she felt that she knew better than anyone else in the group, especially when she had to take group tests, so she withdrew to work on her own. The teachers said that she had a lot to learn from cooperative learning, and they thought it was doing her a lot of good. At the time, Jasmine didn't see this. But Jasmine honored her commitments to classmates when she was in a group situation. She worked very hard in these positions and expected the same commitment from the other students. She was so thorough that she tended to take over and do the work for the others whenever she suspected them of inadequacy.

In the classroom, Jasmine was quietly attentive unless she had not slept the night before or was having "relationship problems," in which case she would appear very distracted. When distracted, she would spend her class time writing notes or daydreaming. Sometimes she would "blow off" a class because she thought she needed some recreation or "fun," so she would just chat with her girlfriends about boyfriends and other girls. She said that was why she had to work so hard at night to keep up with her schoolwork.

Communication didn't cease when the bell rang. Conversations were continued from one class to the next and in the hallways between periods. Personal notes were passed around with regularity. For Jasmine, note writing was a major pastime during class. Boyfriends wrote long letters, which were passed on to Jasmine and her friends via other contacts. Jasmine said:

> Sometimes boyfriends make me feel that I'm taking life too seriously. When I was going out with Chuck, I drove him absolutely crazy with all my meetings and tryouts and banquets. He said, "Jasmine, are you afraid that you're not gonna have enough for college? Why all the activities? I look in your planner to find time for me and you're always busy!" That's when I feel bad about overoccupying myself. I guess I could say that relationships encourage me to maintain an active role in school, but they also set limits.

In her relationships, she tried to encourage the boys to take an interest in school because she knew that she was not going to make anything else her top interest. Most of Jasmine's boyfriends during the time of this study were African Americans. In her campaign speech when she was running for a seat on the student council, she named "improving race relations in the school" as one of her election platforms. Jasmine said that her own family was "very racist," and in some ways she felt she could make up for them with her antiracist stands at school. Jasmine's mother told her to look for brains rather than beauty in a man, because in choosing beauty over brains she had made the mistake of marrying Jasmine's father. From Jasmine's diary:

> The only time a relationship becomes a problem for me is when my boyfriend wants to meet my mom. That's a "no-no." If he can't understand the strict rules under which I live, things just end. Basically boyfriends influence me positively but I rarely have deep relationships because of my mother. I never want to get married, there's just too many problems. Many people are raised to think marriage is so wonderful and I see it as such a burden. I also came across this article where children of broken families tend to carry on getting married and eventually getting divorced, and that is not something I want to go through. . . . I'm not saying that just because the report says that, that it is going to happen in my life, but I realize that I take after my mom in some things that I don't want to.

Because Jasmine's mother didn't allow her to socialize at all outside of school, Jasmine established elaborate schemes to get to see both girlfriends and boyfriends, telling her mother, for example, that she was staying overnight at a girlfriend's house to study. It was the dilemma of deceiving her mother that Jasmine was struggling with at the time she became involved with this study. She said, "There is a monstrous clash of values between me and my mother."

School was Jasmine's life. It was there that she found meaning and engagement. In the first semester of her freshman year, Jasmine scored two As, four Bs, and one C. She was ashamed of this record. She said she got in with

> the wrong crowd, who were smokers and were absent from school a lot. I hung out with those friends for about half the year until I saw what it did to my grades. Then I dropped them. They were kind of curious and thought I was changing, becoming preppy or something. But they weren't really my friends. I never confided in them, and I never trusted them. They weren't losing me and I wasn't really losing them. . . . And you know, I was thinking to myself, "The only way I can help my mom is if I try now, because if I continue to be this way, then it's only going to make it harder for her." So that was my main motivation.

Because she was hanging out with that particular group of friends, her teachers started looking down on her, thinking she was irresponsible. Jasmine missed the recognition from her teachers that she had had when she was younger:

> And what I really missed was being on top, hearing my name in class. That made me feel less important. I wanted to be noticed and stuff. So that summer I took summer school to pull myself up a level in math. You know, my grades came up right away. I started wanting to be responsible and independent. So I went back to my little computer that mom bought me, and I got organized. I joined lots of clubs at school.

Jasmine said that she realized her "mistake" and was glad that she had had the time to pull herself out of the situation she was in and concentrate on her school-work. In the second semester of her freshman year, she made a remarkable academic recovery, scoring five As and two Bs. Since that time, she had scored almost all As, with the very occasional B.

Every one of Jasmine's teachers reported positively on her writing ability. They were also impressed with her organizational skills: "She has such drive, and she is so organized."

Jasmine also entered as many competitions for poster designs as she could. She loved the recognition when she won, which was often.

Tracking, the placement of students in classes according to their level of ability, was something Jasmine approved of. It showed her how far she was from others and how much she had to improve.

Many of Jasmine's conversations were about grades and image. She was overjoyed when she was selected for the National Honor Society. She pointed out that she would have been devastated if she had not been nominated:

> I got into the club, and I was really happy because it wasn't just a club that anybody could join, you know, and I like being in organizations where it's like exclusive, belonging with the elite. . . . I think in levels. When you move down a level as far as success goes, you become really frustrated and discouraged. Being on top of things all the time boosts your ego.

Jasmine said that she liked the system of ranking each person in a grade: "You know where you stand and how much you have to improve."

Jasmine's Relationships with Her Teachers

Despite her high motivation and good grades, none of Jasmine's teachers loved her. They admired her but found her distant and frustrating. There were not many praises for this smart, clever, super-hardworking young woman. One of her teachers said, "I appreciate the fact that Jasmine will come and tell me some of her problems, and I want to be a friend with her. But the next day she'll treat me like dirt! Like I didn't exist! She is very moody."

When she didn't like a teacher she was quick to try to get out of the class. Once when she was unable to transfer, she dropped the class. She said she did this because she often spent the last period with a counselor and had really wanted this class in first period in order to accommodate that: "I needed to talk with that counselor because I could not sit in class with all those problems underneath; I needed to blow it off sometimes." That reason was not conveyed to the teacher, nor did the teacher ask whether there was a particular reason she wanted to change classes. Because of the lack of communication, she was refused permission. She was not one to initiate a conversation unless it was about herself.

Although teachers recognized her abilities, they had unresolved questions about her. When asked why she didn't get more school recognition for her involvements, one teacher said:

I am surprised that Jasmine doesn't get more recognition around the school. She is always doing fantastic work and is involved in everything, but her name is not known. I'll say something about her and the staff ask, "Who's that?" They only know her as the girl with the long hair. Is it because she is Asian or her family is not involved in the school? I don't know.

Jasmine was often absent from class, and because of her absences her teachers were suspicious of her. After one week of tardiness and some absences, a teacher noticed that Jasmine came into class smelling of alcohol. She was taken to the office, and the counselors asked whether she had been drinking. Jasmine replied that she had only gone to the bathroom and put spray on her hair—that was the alcohol smell. The teacher apologized, but Jasmine said that this incident humiliated her, and she was very angry about it. She dropped that class.

The teacher who worked most closely with Jasmine on the school newspaper talked about her frustrations with her: "She is sullen. When she gets rebellious, she won't talk. She gets frustrated at other kids when she works so hard and doesn't see the same commitment on their side. But she is an independent spirit."

School was the place where Jasmine carried on her social life. "At lunch, we like to chat about classes and who is going with whom," and "all that kind of girl stuff," she admitted. Students had only thirty-five minutes for lunch, and because of the school's open-lunch policy, they rushed to their cars or ran up the street if they were going to get lunch at a fast-food store. They ate in less than ten minutes and then drove or walked to a candy store to get the "loot" for the afternoon classes. They arrived back just in time for the next period. Usually Jasmine didn't eat lunch, or she snacked on the way to the library, where she studied or chatted during the lunch period. Her forays to restaurants occurred only when she had money, which was not very often, or when someone else was paying.

The Future and the Now
Jasmine did talk about what she wanted to do when she finished high school. Her mother wanted her to be a doctor, but she was not so sure about that goal because she believed math was her worst subject, and her real interest was journalism. In the meantime, Jasmine was concerned about her grades: keeping her GPA high so that she could get into the college of her choice. She also realized that involvement in extracurricular activities was a means of making contacts and friends and prolonging the school day and putting off going home. One way

Jasmine's mother punished her was by forbidding her to take part in after-school activities, which frustrated Jasmine and occasionally prevented her from taking on leadership roles in group activities. In trying to hide her outside activities from her mother, she practiced what Salzman (1989) called "the art of avoidance and concealment" (123).

Jasmine roller-coastered from highs to lows. The elation at doing something well, receiving acclaim and awards, gave her highs. Being noticed by boys gave her highs. The conflicts with her mother gave her the deepest lows.

The depth of her despair was expressed in a conversation about her attempted suicide, about which she later wrote in the school newspaper. She said:

> I took over twenty Tylenols. It was right after my mom finished yelling at me and speaking about disowning me. . . . If she can't appreciate me for who I am, then I wish she could appreciate me for the person that I'm not: I'm not a druggie, I'm not pregnant, I'm not stupid. She is lucky that she doesn't have a daughter like that. Mom has the biggest attachment to me; especially since she doesn't have a husband, she focuses more on her children. After she finished yelling, I went to the bathroom, and it was like I just decided to give up everything.

Upon finding her slumped over in the bathroom, Jasmine's mother became very compassionate and helped her to the hospital to have her stomach pumped. But after that, they didn't speak to each other for six days. Jasmine said that she never argued with her mother. She just sat and listened to her and let her mother's words run through her head while getting angrier and angrier:

> I guess when you have so much frustration in your life, you can't control your emotions, but one thing you can control is what you learn and how successful you become. So if things get hectic in your personal life, you can kind of make up for it and do things that you can control.

"You are supposed to compromise in life, but with Mom it is always her way," she said. Some months later Jasmine, who was also a peer counselor, decided to put her attempted suicide in the school newspaper: "Many of you must wonder how I can voluntarily put such a personal part of my life in print. It's simple. After having gone through the events of that night, I realize one thing. Suicide is not worth it."

"Some kids said they liked it, and several teachers admired it and thought I was courageous," she said. She was not sure what her mother would have done had she known Jasmine had written it in the newspaper. The perception that she could control her own success within the school environment while her emotional life was "out of control" was the reason Jasmine often talked about her two personalities.

End Thoughts

There are close links between Jasmine's biography and what she did to become successful. Her mother wanted her two girls to become successful through education and to make the most of the educational opportunities for women in the United States. Ogbu (1991) said this was typical of immigrants who come to the United States willingly. They wanted to utilize the new opportunities for success. So Jasmine studied long hours in her own room, which she set up as her place of study.

She was a perfectionist, a great writer involved in many prominent extracurricular activities.

While she acknowledged that relationships were important, she didn't value interpersonal skills, such as working in groups, and she avoided relationships with those who were not interested in school. She had a strong need to be liked but was not sure what that meant in terms of reciprocity in relationships.

Her volatile relationship with her mother encouraged her to succeed and, at the same time, prevented her from doing it the way she thought it should be done. She developed an elaborate network that supported the lies she told to her mother in order to do the things she wanted to do.

Jasmine primarily defined success in terms of getting good grades. She loved streaming (the ordering of students according to performance in a particular subject) and being compared with her peers. "That is what urges me to do better—if I can compare myself with others." But Jasmine's accomplishments seemed to exceed the usual explanations of success.

Some of Powell, Farrar, and Cohen's (1985) key experiences of advocacy, selective admissions procedures, restricted curriculum choices, and guidance in the choice of those subjects, together with high-caliber teachers, helped shape a successful school experience for Jasmine. The advocacy was limited to a few teachers and the social worker, even if she did not form warm relationships with them.

Wanting to take part in as many different school activities as possible brought her involvement in groups as diverse as the cheerleading squad and the National Honor Society. By securing leadership positions in clubs and classroom activities, she achieved her goal of becoming a successful student.

Jasmine said that she had no idols. She didn't watch TV or go to the movies very much, and so the people she admired were in books. She explained, "I like to read stories of people who are trying to overcome things in their lives. They make me realize that things in your life don't matter as much—I mean things in your life do influence you, but the one thing that can really let you succeed is yourself."

Jasmine was oblivious to structural constraints and blamed herself when she was not recognized or rewarded for her efforts (McCarthy, 1993). She was not a popular student with teachers because she did not seek the warm relationships that many other successful students fostered (Davies 1983; Weis 1985a). She expected to be acknowledged and praised for her hard work and her contribution to the school. She couldn't understand why her hard work didn't stand on its own merits.

Chapter 7

Xia: Side Stepping School

It is a warm, wet June night in Plainstown, and approximately 1,500 people are crammed into a local theater for a community musical. There is a huge cast, well over 100. Xia has been selected to play one of the lead roles, a flighty teenager. Her entry comes with a flourish and a vibrancy that this young woman exudes when onstage. Her performance is electric; she lives through the character. The local critics are not slow with their praise, and she rates a special mention the next day in the daily newspaper. (Field notes)

In her diary, Xia wrote:

I was so in love with the cast and crew and show in general—it was a ball! And 1,500 or so people EVERY NIGHT! Wow! That's the most I've ever played for. I was really depressed when it ended. . . . I'll definitely be in the company's future productions. One guy offered me a part in *South Pacific* (he's directing) but I'll be too busy being the scenic artist for *Oliver*.

Xia was recommended as successful by teachers and students. She has been one of the leading characters in the school drama and musical productions the previous year. At school, she was involved in numerous extracurricular activities: she was a peer counselor and a member of the Thespians, the school choir, the National Honor Society, the staff of the school literary magazine, and the staff of the yearbook. She was also a member of a youth advisory board at a local drug and alcohol center, and she worked two nights a week and one day on the weekend at a local restaurant. Xia had a GPA of 4.6, and she ranked in the ninety-ninth percentile in all areas on the national standardized tests, which she had taken each year that she was in high school. Her aptitude score was 141 with 100 being the mean.

She chose Xia as her pseudonym for this research because as she wrote in her diary:

I was given a book by a boy friend called *The Cat Who Walks through Walls* by Robert Heinlein. In it there is an interesting minor character called Xia. The plot is set on the moon where those people not wanted on earth were sent to form a new society. The rules are strict, but they establish a new world full of people of mixed race. I envisioned them being very beautiful and intelligent. I liked the book a lot.

Xia's Schooling

Xia's extracurricular achievements during her junior year were impressive. She had the lead role in the fall play, and the lead in a community musical, and she was scenic designer for another community production, director of the fall class play, and the lead actress in the spring class play. She qualified in the Illinois High Schools Association Speech Tournament and won a Speech Club Varsity Award. Xia's reputation for success was based on her outstanding abilities as an actor and on her high scores on the standardized tests. Some of her activities—participating in counseling sessions, staying at home to complete assignments, or just hanging out with her friends—meant that she was frequently absent from classes. The school records showed that she was absent 27 full days and 60 partial days during the 178 days of school in 1991–92. In order to see how this happened and how she managed to be regarded as a successful student despite it, I spent several days with Xia at school, one of which is recorded here.

A Day in Xia's Life at School

Xia arrived at school at 7:30 A.M. to attend the Thespian bimonthly meeting. The backstage classroom was empty. Gradually, the members of the club drifted in. Xia, ten minutes late, came in with four other students who said they'd been to the doughnut shop "to get the loot." Xia ran the meeting. She was the group's secretary but seemed very much in charge. At the end of that meeting, between leaving the backstage classroom and getting to her locker, Xia gave three messages to different people and asked whether her absence at PE the day before had been noticed—she had skipped class and gone home to complete an essay that was due that afternoon.

We eventually moved on to a physics class. Here the students worked quietly on their homework and prepared for a test to be given the next day. About ten minutes into the class, Xia was called out for a peer-counseling session. She had been a peer counselor since her sophomore year, an activity usually reserved for upperclassmen. Xia, however, was a popular counselor and found herself called on about twice a week to provide counseling for other students. She enjoyed counseling and did not mind missing class to do it. Most of her teachers accepted that Xia chose to do counseling before schoolwork and rarely refused her permission to leave the class.

At the beginning of her PE class, a student approached Xia and told her that she was wanted to work on the school yearbook. Xia smiled, explained to the teacher that, "no, I don't have any other time," and took her leave from PE. Later she explained:

> I have only been to PE about three times this year. I hate it. I don't see why I have to do those physical jerks. I've had a touch of mono[nucleosis] over the last few months, and I don't have any energy for it. Anyway, I want to be the editor of the yearbook next year, and so I want to work on sections of it this year.

At this time, Xia was also preparing for her role as the lead in the upcoming school play. This took a lot of her spare time, both during and after school, and she felt the pressure of it: "One side of my family says, 'Forget about school, and concentrate on the play.' The other side says, 'Forget the play, and concentrate on the academics.' I think I want to forget about school and just do the play, at least until I feel better."

Xia also felt the pressure to do well at whatever she did:

> I think that it goes back to the early days in school. You are not given any basis for feeling good about yourself. It's kind of "Work against each other and see who can be the best, and if you're not the best, keep trying because maybe one day you will be. Keep working harder, keep doing more" instead of, "You're cool the way you are; try to be as good as you can for yourself, not so you can be better than all these other people." At least that is what I think.

At the entrance to the room where the yearbook staff met was a poster that read, A FOOL DOES IN THE END WHAT A WISE PERSON DOES IN THE BEGINNING. Procrastination dogged many students like Xia who were involved in a multitude of activities.

On this day, Xia worked on the layout for the section of the yearbook about the school's musical. She said she liked to do things creatively and a little differently from the way others did them. The teacher in charge of the yearbook commented on the type of student who worked on this project:

> I select the students for the yearbook. They have to be A or B students because basically you put out a two-hundred-twenty-five-page book from August through February, so it is not a therapeutic group—let me put it that way. It

isn't for those failing or not in other activities. It is the top-level kids in the yearbook.

Xia's next period was upper-level French. As we moved to that classroom, Xia chatted with her friends in the hallway. Several students asked her how the play was coming along.

In this classroom, the blinds were drawn, and the students worked quietly. They answered the questions the teacher posed and then took a quiz. Xia sighed a lot and looked at me. At one stage, she asked a question of the teacher, in French. Most of the other students asked their questions in English. I later found out that she didn't attend this class very often. The French teacher said:

Xia can do well. It is easy for her to learn, but she misses so much school that her work is incomplete. I don't know why she is absent so often. I know she is a peer counselor, but keeping track of her is difficult. But because she is bright she makes As and Bs.

She had dropped math this year because she was not getting an A. She explained, "It was too much work, and I didn't want to put in the time with the play coming up."

After her French class, she said she had to go home to finish an assignment due that afternoon. So she skipped choir. At her house, we chatted about assignments, relationships, and control. We sat and talked about the essay she had just completed "An American Hero—Edna St. Vincent Millay." She wrote:

An American hero has spent time pursuing his ideals in conjunction with his struggles to contribute something beneficial and representative of himself and those ideals to society. The contribution of the hero . . . must be a positive influence, as a whole, to American society. This doesn't mean that every individual must be inspired by, reached by, or even familiar with the contributor, but that most of those who know "what he did" have gained something, be it pride in their country from the winning of a war or autognosis aided by the insights of a poem, by the culmination of his "work." Put simply, if you are an American hero, America likes your stuff, and, consequently, likes you.

In her essay, she expressed admiration for Millay because she worked for the suffragette movement, rebelled against the common notions of women as nonintellectual, and asserted herself in her stand for women's equality. Millay's poetry was what Xia liked best, and she could recite whole poems without referring to a book. The idea of emotional distance was evident in the two poems she recited for me.

When discussing her relationships with males, Xia said that she didn't like to become too involved because "I am only sixteen." She saw herself as too young for sexual relations, although she said that the successful students she counseled at school who were involved sexually seemed able to separate their sex lives from their academic lives. She said, "It is the nature of the relationship that can interfere with achievement, rather than sex itself."

Xia liked being smart and in control. "Definitely," she said, "but I like to learn from those I respect."

She said she was prepared to "get on" with those she needed in order to get ahead, for example, by taking a creative-writing class with a teacher she didn't like or by not graduating early so she she could take AP classes, which involve a full year of study but would exempt her from some first-year college requirements.

An example of a time when she didn't feel she was in control was when a friend argued against using school counselors to help with personal problems. He claimed that a student should be able to solve his or her own problems. But Xia believed that the school social worker had shown her a lot of coping skills and had given her a great deal of support throughout her time in high school, and she didn't object to taking advantage of people who offered help. She said that by placing herself in his shoes, she was able to understand why the counselors were not important to him. He had been suicidal while at school and hadn't found the counselors particularly helpful. Xia felt a lack of control during this encounter because she respected her friend but was challenged by what he said.

At the same time that Xia and I were talking about these things, I noted that there were fifteen "house rules" listed on the refrigerator door, one of which was, "Don't feed your friends with my food—Mom!" Most of the other rules related to Xia's doing what she was told by her mother—hours by which to be home and chores to be done around the house. Xia rolled her eyes when I pointed it out and told me to help myself to some food.

We returned to school, and the last two classes of the day were, in Xia's words, "very lively and stimulating." She explained:

> I love these two classes. They are backed onto each other because the teachers are integrating the subjects. If I were to run a school, I would offer lots of combined classes. For me, it is totally ideal. There is time for lots of discussion, and you get to hear everyone's point of view. I would like to have a few classes a day, three times a week or something like that—big assignments, big

papers, big thoughts, and big debates. You learn so much more, and you don't keep on having homework due the next day; you get to take a break from it for a while.

Not having to change to a totally different subject every fifty minutes was a good thing for Xia. She believed she learned more when there was a longer period of time given for the deeper study of a subject. She said that then the students had time to get to know one another better, too.

The class began with the teacher saying, "I don't want to tell you what you have to learn. You have to determine what knowledge you want to have." The topics were chosen by the teachers, but within those parameters the students had a say in what was important to them. The students graded one another from time to time in this class. There was a lot of cooperative learning, and there were group quizzes. In class, Xia began talking about Taoist philosophy, and the other students giggled. One student leaned over to me and said that she thought Xia was "very bright because I can't always understand what she is talking about."

At the end of the day, Xia told me that she was meeting her boyfriend, and she was not going to serve the detention that she had been given for previous instances of tardiness. Her school records noted that on average she missed one or more classes on most days of the last semester. She said:

> One obstacle to my success at school is the attendance requirement. I think there should be an option if you have attained a certain level of study. We should have another system. . . . There is one counselor who is actually pulling me out of classes to tell me that I am missing too much school! I could just shoot him. I'll be going to a class that I don't go to very often, and he'll pull me out and say, "Well, I've written to your parents and they don't call. You're not always excused, and all these teachers are complaining that you're not in class." And I say, "Yeah, yeah, yeah!"

One teacher, however, said that because Xia was away so much, she often had to make up tests when she came back: "She is always excused, and so there is not much that can be done about it. In fact, she may benefit by doing tests after other kids have done them. She has the opportunity to operate that way."

"That sort of comment cracks me up. I hadn't even thought of it!" Xia said when she heard these comments.

Xia in a Major Conflict

In the weeks after the play, which was very successful, Xia began to complain that she no longer enjoyed the theater program. There had been a change of staff, and she clashed with the new teacher, who made a lot of changes in the way things were run. Xia disagreed with her philosophy of including students who missed some rehearsals because of work or sporting commitments. The new drama teacher said:

> When I took this job, the administration told me that there were things that they would like changed about the program. Some of the backstage activities that students engaged in were to be curtailed because they were unsupervised, and I was told to be strict about locking up the equipment. Some of the students didn't like this change in operation.

It was not just the change in operation that caused Xia to fall out with the new teacher, however. She also thought that the new teacher was incapable of upholding the theatrical standards to which she had been accustomed. Xia aggressively put forward her opinion about how the program should be run. The teacher was angry:

> I spoke with Xia. She told me what she thought of the program. I mean she minced no words as far as my ability was concerned. But I have been in the theater longer than she has and worked with a lot of different people. I've also been to school a lot of years to learn my craft, and I'm still learning. And where does this sixteen-year-old girl get off? It hurt! And it divided this group of kids smack down the center.

Xia said that she had told the new teacher her opinion from the beginning, but the problem spilled over when another teacher went to her and reported an overheard conversation, led by Xia, the gist of which was "[These students] are just out to screw the system without giving anything back to it." This teacher blamed Xia for the tensions among some of the upperclassmen. This occurred the week of the auditions for the spring musical. Xia commented:

> It was a terrible week. My mother and I were fighting, and she threatened to kick me out again. I dropped math because it was causing me way too much stress. It was making me sick even thinking about it. And after this teacher reported his interpretation of the conversation we'd had to the drama teacher, what do you know—I didn't get the part. I think I really got screwed over—pardon the expression.

When auditions for the spring musical were held, Xia was listed as a featured character and not as the leading actress. The teacher said that she cast shows based on auditions and Xia had given a very poor audition. Xia said that her performance was much better than that of the girl who got the lead and she was not prepared to accept a lesser role. The teacher explained the situation from her perspective:

> I really wanted her in the show, but if she couldn't be a team player, then we needed to find alternatives. And that is when she came back with my organizational skills and my directing skills and the way the program was being run was not to her liking. And so at that point she didn't need to be a part of it. . . . Xia is the most talented young woman in this school in acting ability. Academically she is gifted. In the fine arts she is gifted. But when we began to have problems, she began to slip academically. And this is directly related to the things she lived for. And that was to perform. When she decided to cut herself off from the program, she had no other outlet. Because of this difficulty, it was very strained in school, and she was looking for excuses not to come.

The impasse between Xia and the teacher existed for several months before both Xia and the teacher, separately it seemed, decided to get some outside intervention. They set up a meeting with a counselor and Xia's mother. This was the first time her mother had been to the school this year. She said:

> It didn't matter who was right and who was wrong. It was one area that I really had to support Xia in because she was down in the dumps, and all of a sudden all these adults and some of her friends, who were supposed to be listening to her, worried her. Also, she has her hands full of her social life, and she wasn't handling the situation very well herself. . . . [Theater] is a goal in my daughter's life, and it was taken away from her. She looked forward to it. It was a devastating event. . . . It was a good meeting. She spoke her mind, and the teacher told her side, and that is what I wanted to hear. In the end, I felt there was room for them to be friends again. It took courage.

In the meantime, Xia had auditioned for a local community-theater production and was given a lead role.

Xia's grandmother said that continual conflict had made Xia a fighter. Having the theater involvement taken from her was a moment of crisis for Xia. She resolved it by bringing together her survival skills: she grieved with her supporters, her grandparents, and her counselors; she drew on her knowledge of the possibilities of counseling in order to fix the situation; and she took herself outside the school and became involved in a local theater production.

The drama teacher said:

I'm sorry that it all happened. But it has been good for her. She thought she could get along without me. She wanted to do her own thing without this department, and I think it has been an eye-opening experience that she can't. There are many outside programs that she can get involved with, but she doesn't get the accolades or the warm fuzzies that people give when they come up to her and say, "You did an outstanding job in that role" or "You were really great" or whatever.

In fact, Xia did receive a lot of accolades and praise for her role in the community production. At the end of the semester, in spite of her frequent absences, tardies, and lateness in handing in her assignments, she made all As and Bs. This was surprising, particularly in choir, where she had missed nearly all the classes in the last three months and had not attended any of the extra-curricular but compulsory activities. On the last day of school, the choir teacher said that Xia was a failure as far as she was concerned. She admitted that she didn't know what to make of her. Yet Xia received an A in this subject on her final transcript. She said that she had spoken to the teacher and arranged to do some work for her later in the year, and so was given the A. Xia could manipulate teachers to bring about academic results even though she had not completed the required work.

The Nature of Xia's Support

By the end of the year, few teachers thought Xia was a wonderful student. Most of them were extremely frustrated by her lack of cooperation, her tardiness, and her absenteeism. She had not given any explanation for this behavior. Several teachers said that if they had known "what the problem was" they might have been able to make excuses for her, but because they had not known what was going on, they had found it hard to accommodate her erratic behavior. Yet even in the two subjects where cooperative group learning was graded, Xia still managed to score an A and a B on her final report card. How did she do this? The teachers knew that she was smart, she handed in enough work to placate them, and the work she handed in was of superior quality. They alluded to the contradiction between her performance and her attendance. Her English teacher commented:

Xia is different. She writes very well. She likes to ride the edge. She likes to take advantage of that, and I don't think she feels at all bad about not being in school. She likes to be selective about what is important for her to study. I have heard her say, "Well, if I'd known we were going to do this, I wouldn't have come to school today."

How did she get away with it when other students would be in the detention room for weeks on end? Her history teacher had said:

> I like Xia a lot. She is a very eclectic person, and she appears to me to be very reflective. She appears to have an easier time stepping into someone else's shoes and seeing how that feels. Maybe she's scoped me out, and she knows what appeals to me, even with a smile or a joke. Like "Oh, Ms. X, I know how you feel about this." And I think she plays that a little. But then I don't feel that she is taking advantage of me. I hear that some of the other teachers are very frustrated with her. I haven't felt that kind of frustration. Maybe she has worked out how to get around me. I'm not sure.

A month later, when I interviewed this teacher again, her attitude had changed. During the previous month, Xia had been absent from her class for over two and a half weeks and had returned without an explanation. She said:

> She came in and wanted her presentation postponed. Frankly, her group presentation had already been postponed because of her absence. Now here she was demanding more time. She does ride the edge. I think she is very used to taking advantage of people. It gets to the point where I am constantly saying, "Why am I giving in to this one person?" That is why it is helpful to have someone remind you of what the problems are so that you can keep them in perspective. But one of my frustrations with the counselors is that they keep the problems to themselves and we don't know what is going on. What I used to think was a real strong ability of Xia's—to step inside someone else's shoes—well, I've seen just the opposite of that. She is very focused on herself and what her needs are.

A ruthless self-centeredness was a common theme among these successful young women. Yet it was not a total focus on the self to the exclusion of others. Xia was also a competent and popular counselor. The frustration for teachers lay in the fact that students were self-centered one moment and then outgoing and considerate at another moment. The English teacher thought that if she had known what the student's problem was, she would have been more lenient with regard to when assignments were due. She was frustrated that she might refer a student to counseling and then never hear anything about that student again. She acknowledged the importance of confidentiality but believed that teachers were often "kept in the dark" about students' problems, and thought this made their job more difficult.

Xia had some strong support among some of the staff. Those involved in the counseling knew of her problems at home and her struggles. One counselor said:

See, unlike many of the teachers, I find Xia absolutely delightful. The fact that she is very capable, the fact that she doesn't fit the mold of sitting through physics and math every day—and with her IQ and her varied interests, I see Xia as a person who is going to be fine. She's left me high and dry from time to time, but she's a very smart girl, and she knows the right moves to make on me. She's apologetic. I think she typifies many actors and actresses that you see on TV; they weren't particularly successful at school, and they had their own interests. If she never took another math or physics class or whatever, she is going to be fine. I just don't think everyone's success has to be marked by getting straight As or Bs in academic subjects. Anyway, she is holding her own. She is doing what she wants to do. She'll make mistakes along the way because she is young. . . . I think to be a little different is delightful.

The administrative dean said:

I don't think there is a pat answer for success. Xia is a bright girl, and because she has made a choice not to get straight As, because she is involved in plays, productions, musicals, and everything else under the sun—she has still had a very successful year. I think if we see success as those forty or so students on the honor role, then we've got a real sick school.

Other staff members outwardly acknowledged Xia as a successful student but saw her drive for perfection as a way of making up for her home situation. Another counselor said:

Xia is driven, and it is not in a healthy way. If you look at her success, it is wonderful in regard to grades or going on to college, but I don't think that she ever feels like she has the true satisfaction with her accomplishments that she should feel. The driving force in her life is the need to be perfect, the need to achieve, and "if I do it right, then I am going to make my family OK." When Xia performs in a play and everyone in the school is telling her how wonderful she was, she doesn't feel that satisfaction because maybe Mom or Dad didn't say—or weren't even there for the performance. Those voices are so much more significant than all the three hundred people in the halls that say, "I'm really proud of you—a wonderful job—you're very talented." I think there is a lot of emptiness about success for these girls. They use excessive activity as a way of diverting or dealing with it. That kind of frenetic activity—on the go, busy, busy, busy—not sitting and taking time to deal with those emotions and feelings that they work hard to get away from.

Xia's Biography

Xia was born in Plainstown, and the sixteen years of her life were spent in the same town and in the same house, a fact she resented. When Xia was ten years old, her parents divorced. Her father remarried and lived with his wife and four stepsons in the same town. Xia saw him frequently and often stayed at their place. Both sets of grand-parents played an important role in her development and network of support. She had one brother, who was younger and lived with her and her mother. The opportunity "to get out of this small town" would not come until she graduated from high school and moved on to col-lege. At least, that was her plan.

Her father and her mother reported that as a child she was "a little precocious, but interested in everything." I asked each of her parents to speak about their memories of Xia as a child.

Her father:

> Xia always had to know more about everything. I don't think she was ever shy. She'd stand nose to nose and still does. She comes by that honestly. When she was about four or five, she was sent to her room for something which she didn't think was right. So while I was eating dinner, she came down dressed for bed, madder than a scalded cat. She lectured me, hands on hips, for about sixty seconds; then she was sent back upstairs. She's ready to do battle.

Her mother:

> She's been outgoing all her life. I'd say it began with the family: my parents and cousins. When she was one, she would put on a show and enjoy the attention. I remember when she wasn't even one, she would do animal noises and get attention; she was awfully cute. She can come back with remarks very quickly, which is not always appreciated by me.

Xia's father graduated from high school and had done a few college courses, none of which he finished. Her mother dropped out of col-lege in her sophomore year but continued her schooling after she married.

Xia's paternal and maternal grandparents lived in Plainstown, near the high school, and Xia regularly dropped by for a chat and advice. Her maternal grandparents paid for Xia to take voice, piano, and swim-ming lessons when she was younger. They took a keen interest in her education and encouraged her to do well, watching her early develop-ment closely.

Her mother commented, "Xia read early. When she started nursery school, at three, she was reading then, I think. But to be honest with you, my mother remembers more than I do. I guess there is an inter-ested grandparent who watched all those things." Her father, in a separate interview, agreed:

She's creative. Everybody promoted her reading, but she did a lot on her own. She liked the Sunday paper, and not just the comics; she had an interest in some of the issues. This was preschool. I'm sure she was reading when she was five, probably earlier than that—the years seem to ram together. She's all arms and legs, gangly, couldn't ride a bike, but she'd sure knock them down with anything else. I did not encourage her in this—no, not really. Maybe softball. The rest is out of my league. I'm not an actor, and I couldn't do the things she does. She's smarter and brighter than I am, quicker on the uptake. But I always tell her that she'll never be as smart as I am.

But her paternal grandmother said that Xia and her father loved performing together:

They like to do different accents, entering right into the character with facial expression and tonal modulation. But there are some of the family [the maternal grandparents] who *push* education. If you got an A and one B, it is like, "Why didn't you get that A?" Or if Xia was in a musical, they would give her vocal lessons and say to her, "with a little more help, you can have the lead role." So it is always "Be the top, be the top." And while that is supportive, on the other hand, Xia resents that. She would say, "Come on, can't you just say, 'That's great that you did this' instead of 'Just a little more and you'd be this'?"

A teacher at Plains High indicated the influence of Xia's father on her: "Her father is a very talented man. I don't know if he has done anything in theater or whether it is in music. But there is a background in performance." Her father had played in a band when he was in his teens.

In contrast with Xia's childhood, her adolescence was fraught with conflict. Over the last few years, the relationship between Xia and her mother had degenerated into a constant fighting. They were intolerant of each other, with Xia refusing to submit to her mother's curfews and house rules. She managed to get her way sometimes with regard to curfews and stayed out as long as she wanted. Her grandmother had offered to have her stay at her house for her senior year so that she would be within walking distance of the school. Xia, who longed to get away from home, declined the offer, saying that she did not want to argue about curfews with her grandparents. That would have destroyed the good relationship she enjoyed with them.

Xia said that alcohol was a problem in her family, especially with her father, so she was scared of it: "I drink sometimes, but I'm frightened what might happen to me if I lost control. Some kids at school drink a lot. My work with peer counseling tells me that."

Her inability to get along with her mother, her father's alcohol problem, and pressure from her grandparents to be the best at whatever she took on led her to seek counseling from the time she entered high school. She frequently tried to get her whole family into counseling, but she said, "it doesn't seem to work." The conflict with her mother had boiled over about two months after we started talking. Xia told what happened:

> Well, the night was really late, and we were fighting all the time. She tried to charge me for picking me up at work. She said I should of taken a taxi. She tried to get money from me, said I owed her for the last three rides—four dollars and fifty cents—and I said, "What are you talking about? You're my mom; you're supposed to do that!" She just started screaming about other stuff and not making any sense. She started calling me crazy and saying that I needed professional help. Then she just started taking my things and throwing them and tearing them up. It's going to sound horrible, but after that I just hit her. I'm not surprised I did it. I'm not proud of that or anything. I wish I hadn't done it because I wish that I had been able to control myself. But I'm not sorry on her account. So she told me to leave and locked the door behind me. . .

> I called some of my friends, and it was obvious that I was upset and I was crying, so they came and picked me up. They were like "Do you want us to call your grandparents? Do you want us to talk to your mom? Do you want us to talk to your dad? Do you want us to call anyone?" . . . And then they bought me dinner and that was real nice. . . . In my groups of friends, everyone's kind of a safety net for everyone else . . .

> I'm done coping!. . . . I've got wonderful friends, but it helps to have a trained professional to help, too. I'm planning on going to see the social worker again. She'll probably have some good insights because I have been talking to her for the past couple of years.

This counseling, Xia admitted, enabled her to see things from the perspective of her parents and others with whom she had conflicts. Over the years, she became a successful negotiator for herself with the skills she learned as a peer counselor and in the counseling she herself received at school.

After a few days, Xia moved back in with her mother.

When asked what being the mother of a gifted child was like, her mother replied:

> It is really difficult. It didn't used to be so difficult, but as she got to be twelve or thirteen, she got to grow up—independent to the point of leaving me out of everything because she thought she could run her own life. It is not so while she is living with me. She just pretends that she doesn't have responsibility to

edition, she said, was a reflection of her, and so she wanted it to be the best.

For Xia, being secretary of the Thespians was a different experience. This group was semi-autonomous and separate from school control. The faculty-sponsor said that it was a student organization, and she had little control over it. Xia liked this independence.

For Alexis, leadership opportunities were provided by her mentors at school. She was asked to lead the "sellout" meeting, which was a high point for her. It was a time when she felt she was able to live out what she'd only heard about from older African Americans who had been part of the civil rights movement. She also took time off from school to attend a march with Sister Souljah, a singer and spokesperson for young African Americans. Whereas the school did not prevent the students from taking part in this event, there was no active endorsement of their participation in it. The students took control of the situation themselves and left school to go.

Taking positions of leadership, or making a stand, was a means to academic success (Garmezy and Rutter 1983). Jasmine, for example, said ecstatically, "Guess what? I've been selected to go to Girls' State. Oh, that is so prestigious; I can't believe that I was selected to go. Only two out of about twenty girls who applied actually get to go, and I was one of them! I'm so excited."

Leadership had benefits other than academic recognition. Emotional satisfaction was important to these young women. The opportunity to participate in a prestigious event made Jasmine very happy because it was an affirmation of her worth and her ability. She believed she was picked because of her work on the newspaper and her participation in so many other extracurricular activities. Thus, her extra time-consuming involvements in leadership paid off with academic recognition and honors.

Three of the girls mentioned receiving emotional satisfaction from leadership positions as an indicator of success. They were happy when they achieved something in the public arena, fulfilling the criterion for success expressed by Jackie—"that they [successful students] learn more and feel good about it."

There is a circular point to be made here. Leadership, for the young women and in the eyes of the school, meant success. Leadership helped them to be perceived as successful, and being perceived as successful enabled them to stretch or break rules and still be accepted. They needed to break rules—for example, taking time off from school—

to get their stressed lives in order. They did this by attending counseling sessions during class time, staying home to nurse a sick parent, visiting a sick friend, avoiding boring classes, or taking time for themselves.

The other side of taking control and assuming leadership positions was excessive activity, or overinvolvement. One administrator said that excessive activity was not good for these young women because it led them to focus on their performance rather than on their inherent value as persons. "They are," she said, "running around seeking attention by doing more and more things which create more stress. They totally overextend themselves." But, as I found out, their excessive activities did have emotional payback. Alexis's engagement in the march with Sister Souljah, for example, left her feeling joyful and empowered. In her diary, she wrote:

> I felt something I have never ever felt before. Joy, respectfulness for my people, and PAIN from walking—Not! These feelings were great to me. Today, on this most historic day that has surpassed all events in my life, I finally understood peace, unity, strength, love and respect that we as African people can have.

It appears that at least three of the young women were not prepared to forgo that which gave their life meaning: involvement in extracurricular activities, or excessive activity, which brought with it engaging relationships and achievements and a sense of belonging. These were all very important to the young women's perceptions of success. Sometimes overinvolvement meant that energy was dispersed over too many activities and their schoolwork suffered. But the perception of success they created by becoming leaders was an important part of their academic success.

Yet this was not the only way these young women became successful students. Jackie and Sabrina, for example, were not in any leadership positions at school. It was not for lack of opportunity; both were offered membership in the prestigious Interact service organization but chose not to accept. For Jackie and Sabrina, the decision not to take part enabled them to focus their attention and time on their paid employment and homework. Like the other three, they made decisions about what activities they did and did not want to be involved in.

Channeling Stress and Anger
The seemingly unrelated-to-success side of these young women's lives is discussed because in studies of successful students an exclusive

focus on strengths sometimes fails to give the full picture, which admits failures and problems. Stress-related illnesses and disorders, such as anorexia, depression, and stomach pains, were frequently manifested in the lives of these young women. They complained of not feeling well and were absent from school often because of stress-related illnesses.

There were many examples of the young women using the problems of their lives to spur them on to success at school. They mobilized their anger and frustration and channeled it into their schoolwork. Jasmine did this when she threw herself into a presentation for her English class on the Monday after being accused of shoplifting. Xia immersed herself in theatrical productions.

At other times, the young women suppressed their stress and anger. Jasmine talked of letting her mother's ranting and raving just flow through her. Alexis went to her room to avoid listening to her parents fighting.

Many times the suppression or the avoidance of stress produced depression, a common thread throughout these young women's lives, which was often referred to by the young women, their teachers, and their friends.

Teachers said to me that these young women were overachievers and that this syndrome was often symptomatic of a stressed home life. There is a parallel with children of alcoholic parents, who are often driven to be the family savior, the one who works hard to try to make up for the shortcomings of the family (Rhodes and Blackham 1987).

Focusing on the Present and the Future
The young women gained credibility among teachers by being hardworking perfectionists who, more often than not, produced high-quality work. They paid attention to detail, both in their personal lives, as evidenced by the number of them who kept lists of things to do, and in their schoolwork, as evidenced by the high-quality presentation of their assignments. Jasmine and Xia had computers at home; Alexis and Sabrina used the school computer; and Jackie had her assignments typed at her father's place of employment when he had work.

Several times one or another of the young women met me at school looking bleary-eyed and very tired and explained that she had worked until the early hours of the morning or stayed up all night to prepare a class assignment. Their attention to detail would not permit them to hand in a shoddy piece of work, and this was appreciated by their teachers. Being hardworking perfectionists meant that they were focused and ignored certain limitations. They were adept at blocking out stimuli that interfered with the task at hand. Jackie exemplified this focus. Her English teacher commented, "She has the ability to exclude other stimuli and focus on a very narrow range of things. . . . She does it when she reads. I've seen her do it in class. She'll be finished her work so she'll just get absorbed in a book, sometimes unrelated to the lesson."

By keeping focused, they were able to see themselves through many difficult times. This ability to focus, along with the other mechanisms they developed for coping with problems at home, resulted in an autonomous approach to their studies (Clark 1983; Rollins and Thomas 1975).

The focus for these young women was graduation. It was the school that coupled "the chance to attend college" with "graduation from high school" as indicators of success, although for Sabrina, graduating was prize enough. The focus on graduation and the attention to detail in their assignments gave these young women the edge in school, while at home these mechanisms helped them block out distractions and tensions.

The future, whether it was seen in terms of graduating and going to college or just graduating, was completely compelling for these young women. Again a parallel: focusing on a bright future is a critical factor in explaining why some children of alcoholics develop into healthy adults (Cameron-Bandler 1986). The only one who mentioned having time for herself now or enjoying the present was Xia. In fact, they all longed to be places other than school; they wanted to graduate; they wanted to go to college and get away from it all.

The protective net that the school offered these young women enabled them to feel secure in what they had accomplished. Whether they will feel as competent in a larger setting, such as a university, is difficult to judge and is not a focus of this study.

Looking to the future is related to "a sense of autonomy and a belief that one can have control over one's environment" (Benard 1992, 4). The sense of autonomy is acted out in taking control of situations. These young women got some control over their stress by absenting themselves from classes and either seeking counseling, resting, or engaging in recreation. They liked leadership opportunities so that they could have control over part of their lives. Taking control gave a certain coherence to their lives (Werner and Smith 1982) and this led to a positive outcome for these young women. This sense of coherence, of purpose and meaning and hopefulness, lay in direct contrast to the "learned helplessness" that Seligman (1975) found in individuals experiencing mental and social problems (Benard 1992).

Establishing Idiosyncratic Credit

What each of these young women did at school was to build idiosyncratic credit from her freshman year on. By building idiosyncratic credit, I mean that they acted in ways that later allowed them to deviate from the norm and still be accepted by teachers and administrators. They showed, over a period of time, that they were capable of doing good work, thereby building up their teachers' high expectations of them. As they began to behave in ways that deviated from the norm, their behavior was accepted or ignored because of the credit they had acquired earlier. By the time they were seniors, they could afford to be a little different, even outrageously different, and get away with it.

Each of these young women had established enough idiosyncratic credit to last her for some time. The fact that they would bend the rules by handing in assignments late or being absent and not get into trouble for it indicated that teachers and administrators perceived them as successful and therefore accepted their behavior. Acceptance of deviance was a support for success.

One prominent example of idiosyncratic behavior is absence from school. Interestingly, most but not all of these students' absences were excused. That meant that a parent or a grandparent had called the school to say the young woman was ill or otherwise legitimately absent. A lot of this absence stemmed from involvement in extracurricular activities (for Xia, Jasmine, and Alexis), or counseling either for themselves or as part of the peer-counseling group (for Xia, Jasmine, and Alexis), and some of it stemmed from their own or their family members' illness (for Jackie, Sabrina, and Xia). Being absent from school or from class often created tensions between the young women and their teachers. Their poor attendance record and lack of responsibility in completing group work on time caused frustration for teachers and classmates, yet they still got good grades. The school's two attendance secretaries reviewed the five young women's records and made a comparison with the "average absences for most students." All the young women were categorized as being absent a lot more often than the average student, who stayed away approximately four to five full days and another eight to ten partial days per year.

Table 1   Days Absent from School

Student	Full Days	Partial Days	Total
Jackie	44	15	59/178
Alexis	12	25	37/178
Sabrina	8	15	23/89*
Jasmine	2	31	33/178
Xia	27	60	87/178
Average student	4–5	8–10	12–15/178

*First semester only.

In contrast, the top five female graduates had very low absentee rates.

Table 1 shows the absences for the five young women and the average student. When the teachers were asked why these young women were allowed so many absences, their answers invariably referred to the fact that the absences were excused and so they couldn't do anything about it. The reasons the young women gave for their absences centered on their activities elsewhere: Jackie stayed home to look after her mother; Jasmine and Alexis attending other school-related-functions, including counseling sessions; Xia was, first, involved in extracurricular programs, such as the peer counseling, and second, making time for herself and her out-of-school friends.

None of the young women served a detention in the year of this study. All of this required the cooperation of the administration, and generally the young women were adept in gaining that. They were manipulators of the system. Many other students would not have been able to gain this cooperation. Manipulation of adults or the ability to find and gain adult supporters was a feature of these young women's lives.

One reason these young women received seemingly unqualified support from teachers was that they appeared to be mature. Each of them was mature beyond her years. All of them viewed themselves as more mature than their peers and were regarded by teachers and peers as being more mature.

For teachers, maturity was the ability to relate to adults; it was being known as "sensible." Typical of comments by teachers is one made about Jackie. "Jackie is a very complex young lady . . . maturity-wise, she is beyond most of the students in [AP English]." A teacher said about Alexis, "The other girls in the cheerleading squad are not like her. They are high school girls, whereas Alexis is much more able to relate to those older than her. I think she is more mature and sensible."

These young women also liked teachers and administrators to treat them as adults. They responded favorably when they received respect, which they interpreted as being treated as an adult. When they were treated as children at school, they either actively tried to reframe the situation to their own liking, sat passively, or skipped class. Perceiving themselves to be adult, mature, and responsible for their own decisions enabled them to work the school system to their advantage.

For the young women, being adult and mature meant making decisions about which school regulations to follow without being unduly worried by what the school authorities thought of their behavior. Xia reacted to an administrator who called her out of class to discuss her absenteeism by commenting, "I could just shoot that administrator; he's always annoying me. He is irrational. Obstacles need to be taken care of if they are in the way of a goal, so nothing will stop me." Xia's attitude was to place herself outside the school rules, particularly with regard to attendance; she created the perception of herself as beyond school rules.

Of the five young women, Sabrina was the only one who openly admitted that she didn't want to cause trouble for the faculty. She wanted the teachers to maintain their positive attitude toward her, and she did this by being compliant. Sabrina accepted the teachers' perception of her as a successful student.

Although teachers agreed that these young women took advantage of opportunities, they did not always agree that the decisions they made were beneficial to their education, especially with regard to absenteeism. Nonetheless, having teachers whose attitude toward them was positive was one of their recipes for success.

For Xia and Jackie, being mature sometimes meant feeling different from others, a feeling that in adolescence was a characteristic of the smart and gifted women studied by Kerr (1985). Jackie showed her difference from her classmates by refusing to dress and act like them; she wanted to be different. Xia never discussed being different; she knew she was different, and she liked it.

Being different and being happy with the difference contrast with being different and wanting to change the state of affairs. Jasmine, Alexis, and Sabrina worked hard at not appearing to be different, but these three were the ones who were visibly different. Jasmine's ambition was to become "just like an American citizen." She knew the ways in which she differed. Alexis fought the way in which she was perceived as being different, which in the school manifest itself in racism against African American students. Sabrina hated being singled out as a special-education student. The teasing and accusations angered her. She didn't want to be different. She wanted to show others that she was as good as they were. Her way of doing this was to get A grades even if that meant taking the lowest-level classes.

These positions on difference reflect the differing perceptions of what it takes to be successful. The young women's handling of the public perception of their differences secured respect. This was because each student used the strengths of her difference to establish idiosyncratic credit. The very point of this discussion is that in each young woman's difference lay her strength; each young woman used her difference from the mainstream to create a new way of being a successful student.

In summary, these explanations for academic success focused on the self-as-agent in the contexts of school and family. It was responsiveness to opportunity that made these young women successful. They took control of their own learning situations, used opportunities for leadership as a means to being seen as successful, channeled their stress and anger into schooling, and focused on perfection while ignoring their limitations, thus pushing themselves on to success. They were supported by establishing idiosyncratic credit, which enabled them to deviate from expected norms without retribution.

The Way the Families Functioned to Achieve Success

Many studies show the close connection between family support and school success (Betz and Fitzgerald 1987; Clark 1983; Danziger and Farber 1990; Sewell and Hauser 1975; Steinberg, Elmen, and Mounts 1989). In the comparison study of the top five female graduates at Plains High, I found this to be true. All of these young women cited their parents as being heavily involved in their studies and being their greatest support. In a personal communication in 1992, I was warned by Spender that the study of success and stressed families would be sad and possibly an example of hegemony at its best. Spender was referring to the obvious explanation for success at school as being that the young women who succeeded would have rejected their families in order to incorporate themselves into the dominant school culture of academic success. Contrary to this expectation, however, I found hope in the fact that, notwithstanding the stressful family lives led by the young women in this study, they were successful at school and, with the exception of Sabrina, showed no signs of rejecting their families. The existence of either severe or mild family problems—such as physical abuse, alcoholism, or other substance abuse, attempted suicide, poverty, or divorce—were not in themselves deterrents to academic achievement. In fact, the way the young women developed coping mechanisms within their stressed families transferred to the success scenario.

Clark (1983) found that a toughness was required of girls, as well as boys, if they were to achieve academic success: "The toughness required for girls to be academically successful results not from parental support, but from the lack of it" (197). In Clark's study, that toughness was gained from ghetto living. The toughness required to succeed at Plains High was developed in response to the problematic conditions under which these young women lived; it was a by-product of the autonomy, strength, and self-agency that the young women developed so as not to let these conditions overwhelm them. Also, however, these young women had supportive factors at school and at home to help them achieve success.

Rutter (1984) found gender to be a protective factor in resilient children but didn't say why this was so. In this study, I found the young women were given tremendous responsibilities within their families because they were women. They were responsible for supporting the family or themselves financially; they gave moral support to their parents; they were the family's hope when things seemed very bad. The traditional idea of the dutiful daughter seemed to hold in most of their families. While these extra responsibilities caused considerable stress, they also gave the young women a sense of autonomy. Because they could not rely on their parents for academic support, they were their own agents in finding support in their teachers and in activities at school.

In both Jackie's and Jasmine's families, there was a strong belief that women were not only equal to men but in many ways a lot better than they are when it comes to school success. Jackie had five brothers who did not complete either high school or college; she was the one her parents expected the most of academically. Jasmine was constantly reminded that if she were back in Southeast Asia, she would be tilling the fields while her male cousins were pursuing their education.

This served as a goad to her performance. Xia had one brother and four stepbrothers, all younger than she, and she was the star performer when it came to academics, according to one of her grandmothers. Sabrina and Alexis were expected to be better than their older siblings, who had either not graduated from high school or dropped out of college. Sabrina was expected to obtain loans for her bankrupt brother even though she was working only part-time and had very limited resources. In fact, all five families were very demanding of their daughters in many ways. How the attitudes the girls developed at home transferred to their academic aspirations is clear in the following example of the study of mathematics.

None of the young women was interested in pursuing a career in either math or science despite the good standardized test scores they received in these areas (with the exception of Sabrina). It has been said that women tend to pursue nontraditionally female occupations if they are encouraged to do so by their fathers (Wilson, Weikel, and Rose 1982). I found this to be true of the top female graduates surveyed, who said that their fathers were significant supporters in their education. None of the five young women in this study had fathers who encouraged nontraditional careers, although Alexis's father encouraged her to study business in college. Jasmine's mother wanted her to be a doctor, but Jasmine believed that her math scores were not good enough. The careers the young women in this study planned were generally traditionally female. Their successes were in traditionally female areas.

According to Benard (1992), within the risk environments protective factors can co-exist. Whereas within the stressed families several protective factors appeared to work for these young women, just three are discussed here: the family's belief that education is important, the contradictory nature of the parent-daughter relationships, and the extended family as a safety net.

The belief that education is important as a means of advancement is one of the few things common to all the families in this study. Jasmine's mother was emphatic that her daughter not end up like her, with no education. Xia's father and mother just expected her to go on to college, and a good college at that. Jackie's mother was emphatic that her only daughter do what she wanted at college. Alexis's parents punished her when she started "messing up her grades," and they provided her with the financial resources to go to college. Sabrina's parents wanted her to graduate early so that she could move into the workforce and support herself financially. There was no indication that any of these parents would have accepted their daughters as drop-outs. In fact, the evidence strongly suggests that they would not have tolerated such behavior. High academic expectations on the part of all the parents influenced the girls, giving them the impression that even if they stayed away from school, they couldn't allow themselves to get low grades. Fear of bringing home a bad report card motivated them to do well. This finding supports Connell's (1985) argument that work-ing-class families do have educational expectations of their children; they are just expressed differently from those of middle-class parents.

All the families also made rules to ensure their daughters' academic success. Having high expectations and rules did not mean that the rules were applied consistently. Jackie stayed out after finishing her shift at the gas station at midnight. Her mother rationalized this by saying that she had to have some time for herself. Xia fought with her mother, usually over curfews and house rules, which she ignored or deliberately disobeyed. Her mother threw her out of the house when she could no longer control her daughter. Sabrina, Jasmine, and Alexis experienced severe discipline and irregularly applied rules. These three reported being physically abused. Jasmine had the most regimented house rules of the five young women, and they were so strict that she devised elaborate ways of getting around them. But all these families' rules, while often flouted, show the importance the families placed on education.

Family inconsistency in establishing rules and meeting out punishments is supposed to be among the reasons why students do not do well in school. This is a common myth among teachers and research-ers (Baumrind 1978; Fowler 1992). I found that the autonomy, men-tioned earlier, developed by responsibilities at home, contributed to the girls' independence at school. They seemed to want to keep up their academic performance in order to keep their parents happy and to please themselves.

The families also provided some basic resources. All the young women had a room of their own where they could study. A quiet place to study is a factor in success at school (Clark 1983). Students who have to share a room with siblings or who have to work in a noisy area of the house find it difficult to concentrate on their work. The provi-sion of educational resources in the home was a result of the young women's agency within their families, too: they often told me that they had had to ask for the resources; their parents didn't just provide them. In obtaining these resources, the young women were acting as agents for themselves.

The parents left it to their daughters to seek specific guidance from the school in regard to the classes their daughters should take, career counseling, and procedures for taking tests and applying to college. It is often in these areas that parents flounder. They have not been to college, and so they do not know the procedures or deadlines for applications. Once again, these young women stepped in and took the responsibility upon themselves. They chose the classes they wanted, checked out the school handbook to determine course levels and grade weighting. Most times they talked their options over with administrators or counselors. The young women's responsibility in getting the information they needed was crucial. Sabrina did not have an intense desire to find out about college, and her resistance to her mother's insistence that she go was shown by her not getting the information she needed in time to apply.

According to Clark's (1983) list of seventeen success-producing patterns in high achievers' homes (202–03), these five young women did not compare favorably. As Table 2 shows, the parents expected the students would take responsibility for their own education and graduate.

Clark said that the fewer of these factors present in a child's life, the less likely he or she is to succeed. It is difficult to know why so few of Clark's criteria for high achievement apply to these five young women. What the comparison does show is that despite the stressors in the families of these young women, there were some supports, and these enabled them to gain stability and see a certain coherence in their lives.

Generally, one would describe the nature of these young women's relationships at home as distant and nonsupportive of academic success. The parents never attended parent-teacher evenings at the school and only one parent, Jackie's mother, spent time helping with homework. This distance between parent and child reinforced the young women's sense of independence and autonomy, which they applied to their learning situations.

The young women's relationships with their parents varied in intensity and closeness. Xia's constant battles with her mother reflected their lack of communication. Sabrina's hatred of her mother's drunkenness became a hatred of her mother. She loved her father, and even though she said he was weak for not leaving her mother, she acknowl-

Table 2   Success-Producing Patterns in High Achievers' Homes

Pattern	Jackie	Alexis	Sabrina	Jasmine	Xia
1. Child has had some stimulating, supportive schoolteachers.	x	x	x	x	x
2. Parents have initiated frequent school contact.					
3. Parents are psychologically and emotionally calm with child.					
4. Child's psychologically and emotionally calm with parents.					
5. Parents expect to play a major role in child's schooling.					
6. Parents expect child to play a major role in her schooling.	x	x	x	x	x
7. Parents expect child to get post-secondary education.	x	x	x	x	x
8. Parents have explicit achievement-centered rules and norms.					
9. Child's long-term acceptance of achievement norms shows she views them as legitimate.					
10. Parents establish clear, specific role boundaries and status structures with themselves as the dominant authority.			x	x	
11. Siblings interact positively as a structural subgroup.					
12. Conflict between family members is infrequent.					
13. Parents frequently engage in explicit achievement-training activities.					
14. Parents frequently engage in implicit achievement-training activities	x				
15. Parents firmly and consistently monitor and enforce rules.				x	
16. Parents provide liberal nurturing and support.	x				
17. Parents defer to child's knowledge in intellectual matters.				x	
TOTALS	5	3	4	6	3

edged that he was a strength for her. Alexis's parents fought so much with each other that she felt "out of the family relationship." Jasmine desperately wanted to relate to her mother and was often seeking ways to make her mother notice her; other times she just wanted her mother to leave her alone.

These young women suppressed pain and anger often in order to have some stability in their lives, to give some coherence to what was generally a chaotic situation. Indeed, intimate connection to others is often a source of pain (Salzman 1989). But in these cases, it was a pain the girls were prepared to put up with rather than lose the fractured relationships they had. Sabrina was the only one to leave home of her own volition during the course of the study. Xia chose to stay with her mother rather than live with her grandparents because she did not want to negotiate with her grandparents for the freedoms she had already won from her mother. Jackie was the exception. In fact, her close relationship with her family was cause for concern among some of her teachers: they thought that she was sacrificing her own young life for the sake of her parents. One teacher said she had concerns that the relationships within Jackie's family were not healthy in that the parents were too dependent on their daughter.

One important feature of stability in these young women's lives was the access they had to their extended families for moral and financial support. Each of them had grandparents, aunts, uncles, cousins, or older siblings that they interacted with on a regular basis, some more than others. Until her grandmother's death, Sabrina found strength in her support and love, even though she did not see her very often. Xia's grandparents were her listeners and supporters when she called in on them, which was almost daily. Jasmine had aunts, uncles, cousins, and a grandmother who lived on the same street. Her grandmother looked after the girls when their mother was sick. Jasmine said that her cousins were mostly boys and they did very well at school. She had one female cousin, who was not very interested in school, and Jasmine did not respect her for that. She believed that this cousin was continuing the traditional Southeast Asian woman's role that her mother had always scorned. Alexis's extended family was very important to her but an ambivalent support for academic success. Because she lived in a wealthier neighborhood, her aunts and uncles had to be convinced that she was not a sellout. They were not so much involved in encouraging her to achieve at school as they were in helping her build her identity as an African American. And it was for her support of the African American identity that Alexis gained a lot of her prominence and success at school.

The extended-family support thus enabled the young women to survive and lift them up in times of crisis at home. The presence of extended-family members, with their demands and their supports, acted as an emotional safety net for some and as academic encouragement for others. However they are defined, both the emotional support and the academic encouragement helped the young women achieve academic success.

So how did these families work for academic success? Each family believed that education was important, even though this belief did not result in positive intervention in their daughter's education. Sometimes punishments were incurred if poor report cards were brought home. Each young woman had educational resources at home, especially a quiet place to study. In all the families, gender was regarded not as a barrier to education but as a goad and a strength. There is evidence to suggest that being a female in these families actually added to what was expected of these young women. These protective factors in the stressed families worked to support the educational aspirations of the young women.

The Way the Students Worked the School to Achieve Success

Learning the Politics

The political environment of Plains High was created by the persons who made up the school and by all that they had done to "make a place for all" (Plains High principal). The politics of success was embodied in the teachers' and the administrators' values, which they expressed in what they did and did not do in areas that affected the students. Success was also affected by the students' responses to the school. If the students learned what the school valued and if they knew how to make that knowledge work for them, then they would be successful. If they did not learn the system, they failed or were ignored.

The formal culture of the school operated to uphold very traditional values. Honor rolls, tracking, honor-society inductions for the academic elite, awards nights, and AP classes were all important. What the teachers valued was communicated by their actions, as can be seen by the fact that more than twenty-five faculty members attended the Awards Night, and about the same number attended the National Honor Society induction. At two much larger gatherings of students and their families, the annual Choral Night and the African American Talent Show, fewer than five faculty members who were not involved in organizing the event were present. Knowing what teachers' valued and emphasized was important to success as it was defined by the school.

One way of gaining respect was by being seen as having ability, and having ability was demonstrated by joining clubs, taking AP classes, and doing high-quality work. Those who gained the respect of the teachers did not get many detentions or suspensions. The young women's idiosyncratic behavior was generously tolerated.

Knowing what was acceptable, gaining the teachers' respect and being viewed positively were part of being successful. Also part of being successful was performing in public, for example, by acting in a play or speaking before a group. The young women who used this method to achieve success were reinforced in their beliefs by the accolades they received. Again, teachers respected ability. By gaining a teacher's respect for her ability, a student could gain respectability. "Having the teachers positive toward you was a factor in success," said Jackie.

A further political act was the young women's relationships with their teachers and peers, which were protective of academic achievement. The young women associated with and learned from those teachers who related to them as "friends" (Jackie), as "moms" (Alexis), as "people I respect" (Xia), as "someone you can touch base with" (Jasmine), as "helpers" (Sabrina). All of the young women, except Jackie, indicated that their relationships with their teachers were different from those with their parents. The ones with their teachers were more adult. They were also more profitable in terms of academic success, although generally they were not deep attachments of the mentoring type. Alexis and Xia did form a trusting and close relationship with one of the counselors. Jasmine used the same counselor on many occasions but never referred to her as a friend.

It would seem that these young women cast their teachers in the role of provider. They wanted them to provide intellectual help, to pass on to them the skills they did not already have, to show them how to write and think. They saw this as the teachers' duty. These expectations were generally accompanied by appreciation when the expectations were met: the young women expressed gratitude toward and satisfaction with teachers who did their jobs effectively—but they were quick to criticize those who did not. They stayed away more often from classes they thought were not intellectually stimulating or beneficial. When a teacher showed a personal interest in them, they reciprocated by making an extra effort in class and voluntarily explaining their absences. There was no doubt that these young women sought out teachers with whom they could establish good working relationships, although there was variation in their approaches. That is, the young women approached the teachers variously as friends, helpers, persons to touch base with, mothers, or persons to respect.

With their peers, the young women tended to end relationships that they found did not support them in their goal of academic success. This didn't mean they didn't establish nonprofitable relationships; on the contrary, they seemed to do so often. Several of the girls received counseling for the destructive nature of some of the friendships they did form, and they often laughed over the "little red flag" that signaled a bad relationship. The "little red flag" was a term used by the counselor to mean "wake up, understand and recognize the signs of a bad relationship." What all of them did was end the relationships when it became obvious that they were not beneficial to their success.

Although these young women's relationships were for the most part emotionally distant their diaries revealed a longing for the close attachments they did not have. Yet their lack of emotionally involving relationships also gave them time to focus on their schoolwork. The difference between them and the other young women I interviewed as a comparative group—young women with good test scores and poor records of performance—was in this matter of relationships. The three young women who were not doing well at school had strong attachments—to a boyfriend, a child, or a group of friends who were not interested in academic success at school. The five young women in this study, however, had complex relationships. On the one hand, they were characterized by emotional distance, which worked in their favor by allowing them to concentrate on their schoolwork. On the other hand, I found that when Xia and Alexis formed attachments to their friends outside school, their schoolwork suffered. Noting the "red flags" the young women moved from attachment back to distance, which enabled them to remain focused on their aim of graduation.

Tapping into the Learning Environment
As described in chapter 2, there is an academic elitism in operation at Plains High. From this academic environment come most of the prizes

meted out at Awards Night, the possibility of attending a prestigious college, and leadership positions in the school. In tapping into the learning environment, the young women bought into the "special" side of Plains High (Powell, Farrar, and Cohen 1985). They selected classes whose teachers they knew brought the curriculum alive, they made friends with teachers who "cut the slack" for them, they used the counseling services, and they seized opportunities for leadership in class and in extracurricular activities. They uncovered the caring side (Noddings 1984, 1988) of Plains High, which was made up of people who understood and worked with the realities of these young women's lives. Some faculty members moved beyond what was required of them in order to support and help in any way they could. These caring people were very important to the success of the young women in this study. Two significant ways in which staff members manifested the caring side of Plains High were in cutting the slack for students and in providing counseling.

Cutting the slack occurs when a teacher bends the rules for a student whom the teacher knows is genuinely disadvantaged by school rules and regulations. This notion relates to and is an extension of idiosyncratic credit. There was a tacit belief among some staff members that "a little difference is delightful." Unspoken permissions, even if they went along with frustrations, were granted to students so they could control their lives, as long as they did not disturb the general body of students.

What do teachers do when a student has to work until midnight and comes to school very tired with work unfinished? Jackie was the most obvious example of a student whose teacher cut the slack for her during the first period of each day when she was meant to be a TA. She was often absent and yet the teacher, knowing that she had worked until midnight the previous night, did not mark her absent. Other teachers also bent the rules in accepting late assignments from her. Although detentions were the usual punishment for those who broke the rules in Jackie's case tardies and undone homework assignments were just not investigated.

When a student found a teacher who understood the stressors in her life and adapted the program accordingly, this made for success. Success for the young women in this study meant seeking out teachers who cut the slack for them. The teachers allowed these young women a lot of freedom to take control in these situations even if that meant the teachers risked being censured by the administration. Students who did not have the capacity to form trusting relationships that led to the slack being cut found it difficult to succeed at school.

For example, Cassie found that the ability to establish good relationships with teachers who would cut the slack for her was missing. After having been away for three months for the birth of her baby, Cassie described her experience of returning to school, as a "wall of silence." The teachers and administrators referred to her as having committed "academic suicide." It seemed that the teachers would cut the slack only for those they saw as deserving, those whose stress circumstances were "beyond their control." The five young women in this study fell conveniently into this category. It was obvious that when Xia began taking too many days off of her own volition, the slack was not taken up as enthusiastically as it had been before. Teachers often said to me that they would be willing to make concessions for students who let them know their circumstances. But because they didn't know what Xia's problems were, they felt their "hands were tied."

Part of this "not knowing" was an administrative procedure in that teachers would not automatically be told by the attendance office the reason for an absence; they had to find out themselves. If students were "excused," meaning they were listed as having a legitimate reason for their absence, the teacher was not required to take action. If the students were "unexcused," meaning their absence was not authorized, then the teachers had some power to intervene. For the young women in this study, tapping into the learning environment meant establishing relationships with teachers who would make allowances for deviance and with peers who didn't interfere with academic success.

Once again the study of mathematics serves as an example, here as a further example of a barrier to tapping the learning environment at Plains High. All five young women in this study had difficulty finding a math teacher with whom they could communicate. None of them perceived herself as a good mathematician, yet all but Sabrina had above average standardized-test scores in math. All reported that math was their major problem subject. Given these standardized-test scores, their complaints, and problems with the math instruction they received, it is significant that they did not, in fact, do better than they did. In the year of this study, math grades at Plains High were lower than the grades in other core subject areas. More students failed math than any other subject, and fewer students got As in math, indicating that the math teachers marked much harder than the English, social studies, or science teachers. Two administrators told me that this discrepancy had been noted, and the faculty had been told to examine the situation. Changes in staffing and teaching methods were planned for the following year.

The point at issue for the young women was that math was the one area in which they were unable to tap into the learning environment. When communication and respect were absent, the students found success more difficult to achieve. The five young women in this study were able to ignore problems in other subjects but were unable to do so in math. Ignoring barriers in this situation was not enough; they needed some other supports in order to succeed. They didn't have the financial resources to be tutored, as other students did, nor did they have parents who emphasized math over other subjects. And they did not find teachers who would cut the slack for them here. Also, the linear setup of the math curriculum required regular attendance, so here their frequent absences worked directly against them.

A way in which four of the five young women in this study tapped into the learning environment was by using the services of the Counseling Center during their final year at school. Having someone who took the time to deconstruct their negative past experiences and helped them see how their behavior was influenced by these events was an important service. The overextended services of the Counseling Center at Plains High ran individual and group therapy sessions that enabled many students to begin the process of reviewing their lives and placing the stressors they experienced in some perspective. Participation was voluntary, and four of the young women in this study seized the opportunity. The counselors' approach was to get students in counseling to see their families as separate from themselves and to make decisions about appropriate responses to problems from a reconstructed knowledge of what was happening in the family. This removal of themselves, although hypothetical, helped participating students develop a certain autonomy. Several times these young women asked their parents to join them in counseling. The parents either refused or went once and did not return. The counselor regretted this because she believed that everyone had to be involved if the families were to be helped with their problems. She reflected:

> That is one of the limitations of this job. You can't get the families to participate, and you can't force them. The best solution is get the girls to cope the best they can. It is not the ideal. Nothing ever is. But this is something that will be ongoing with them. It will always come back to learning to nurture and care for themselves and to accept themselves as they are, to appreciate who they are, which is a really different thing from what they are used to [getting from their families].

Learning about and valuing autonomy reinforced the students' view of themselves as adults making their own decisions. It was here, in the counseling sessions, that they learned about the "little red flags" indicating a bad relationship. They learned to accept what they couldn't change and to act when they could take control of their lives. The four young women who availed themselves of the counseling services at Plains High said that counseling was a very positive influence on their lives.

These young women worked the school for their success. They learned the political setup of gaining credibility early so that if they slacked off, they could rest on their laurels for a while. They gained respectability through extracurricular involvement and high-quality work. They established profitable relationships with faculty members and peers, and they cut loose those relationships that interfered with their long-term plans. Although they maneuvered themselves into some productive classes, there was a barrier in their math classes. They didn't have the protective factors in this area that they were able to muster in other areas. They tapped into the learning environment. They fought their way into good classes and made friends with those who would support them and understand their backgrounds. Others used leadership positions to try as many experiences as possible. They wanted to learn, and more than that, they wanted to do well. They associated with friends who supported their efforts. They affiliated with the academically advantaged and effectively used the counseling and guidance services offered by some competent and caring staff members.

The school motto, "Let us boldly pursue success and excellence for all," worked for these young women. But as the teachers pointed out to me at the very beginning of the study, "These are not your usual success stories." Why they are not is not difficult to imagine. The usual success story at Plains High is the story of privilege and elitism. These stories underscore the work that has to be done by other young people and the help they need from their teachers if they are to succeed at school. They have to become their own agents and seize the many opportunities that exist at school. These young women had families that, according to all the usual measures, did not meet the criteria for the production of successful students. But within these stressed families, we see many supportive factors. At school, the young women learned the political setup and tapped into the learning environment. A few caring and supportive adults in this setting made it possible for them to do that.

Chapter 9

Success at School

Success is learning more and feeling good about it, having good letter grades and teachers who have positive attitudes to you. (Jackie)

Success means understanding and applying what you are taught to life. (Alexis)

Having A-pluses is success. Some people think if you did your very best, you should have an A. Getting a C means you have to study harder. (Sabrina)

To me, academic success is synonymous with scholastic achievement, the ability to acquire instructional material in a way that can be integrated, regurgitated, and applied to life. Academic success means to maintain above-average marks, to apply oneself to different elements/institutions in society, and to set personal standards/priorities by looking at the way one has been taught/raised. But of foremost importance, to do all of this and be content. (Jasmine)

You are academically successful when you possess the desire to learn not for the grade on the transcript but for personal growth. Success is in the desire to grow, not necessarily attaining the final result, . . . trying, wanting to do well, wanting to be the best you can. (Xia)

Let us boldly pursue success and excellence for all. (Plains High motto)

There is nothing extraordinary in these statements. One would expect young women to make such statements. What is extraordinary are the young women who made them and how they went about realizing their desire for success. These "success is" statements recapitulate the meanings that the five young women in this study gave to success. They are not that different from what most smart students generally want, and therein lies the question. Should they have been different? Is it a surprise that these smart young women sound like any other smart young women?

The differences between them and other smart young women lie not in their expectations but in how they went about becoming successful at school. It is evident from the many comments by their teachers that course requirements will be adjusted if the teachers know the circumstances of their students' lives. There is a fine line, however, between adjusting course requirements and lowering standards. Most teachers would deny that they were lowering standards when they adjusted requirements, and these young women wanted to achieve just like the others; they did not want their teachers to lower their standards so that they could achieve.

The students in this study placed emphasis on grades, on having teachers who were positive toward them, on working hard themselves, on doing their best, and these qualities reflected what they thought success was. What differentiated them from the students in the comparison studies was not just how these students went about becoming successful, but the fact that certain factors in their lives necessitated them using a different route to achieve success. And what differentiated them from others who did not achieve success were having extra responsibilities at home, having focus, having the ability to build idiosyncratic credit, and having teachers who cut the slack. They were resilient, tough young women. Their resilience came from a combination of past and present strengths, protective factors, and their hopes for themselves in the future. What they aspired to differed little from what many other successful, smart students aspire to. What was different was that they went about becoming successful in ways that were different from the ways of those who did not have multiple stressors in their lives. The creation of different pathways to success is important to understand. The more that diversity is recognized, understood, and promoted, the more students will succeed.

A Review

This research fulfilled a need for a more integrated approach to the study of success across the contexts of family and school (Benard 1992) and a call for more study of the strengths of resilient children (Garmezy 1992) and in particular, resilient young women (The resilient woman 1992). There were young women at this school who were academically successful and yet had a lot of stress in their lives. I was committed to finding out how they succeeded. What were their supports and strengths in both the family and the school?

This study of success at school was influenced by both gender and race. Nonetheless, contrary to the predicted outcomes of Fennema and Sherman (1978), who found socialization to be a debilitating factor in school success, I found that for these young women, socialization was a positive factor in their success. The toughness required to meet their responsibilities in the family was transferred to the school setting, where the young women focused on their work, organized themselves, and took advantage of the opportunities offered by the school for involvement. There was congruence with the findings of previous gender research (Sadker and Sadker 1982) in the fewer resources for girls, especially in community-sponsored activities, such as Girls' State, and in organized sports. The traditionally female role of supporting male sports activities is still, to some extent, in operation at Plains High, with girls having fewer options in sports than boys. In the level-three classes (advanced), girls had the same access as boys. That these young women chose traditionally female careers is consistent with the findings of Wilson and Boldizar (1990). But their achievement in mathematics was inconsistent with their ability levels, as indicated by their scores on the standardized tests. Why this was so is beyond the scope of this study. The reproduction of the "gender regime" by teachers and parents at Plains High was consistent with the findings of Kessler et al. (1985).

The challenge to diversify the curriculum (McCarthy 1990), and not to lower standards, for the increasing numbers of students from nonwhite backgrounds was requested by several students at Plains High. African American student leaders asked for an upgraded literature program that addressed current issues, and a course on Native American culture was requested by Jackie. The laying off of African American faculty members in late 1992 was seen by students and the African American community as a failure of the school to meet the requirements of the district's affirmative action policy. For African American students, who constituted the largest minority group at Plains High, there was little instruction, either in content or in teaching methods, that directly addressed their lifestyles.

The Families

In each of the biographies, there was a significant event or series of events that disrupted the life of the young woman and her family. For Jackie, it was the retrenchment of her father's employment and the family's being thrown into poverty. For Alexis, it was the conflict of growing up African American in a predominantly white society that sees itself as the norm. For Sabrina, it was her mother's ongoing alcoholism and its effects on her. For Jasmine, it was the experience of being a refugee and growing up in a new country that offered many opportunities. For Xia, it was the alcoholism and stress in her family, which contrasted with her own desires for herself. Experiences like these turn lives around and have effects at the deepest levels. Even when interpreting the particulars of an individual life, Denzin (1989b) said that

> there is no clear window into the inner life of a person, for any window is always filtered through the glaze of language, signs, and the process of signification. And language, in both its written and spoken forms, is always inherently unstable, in flux, and made up of the traces of other signs and symbolic statements. Hence there can never be a clear, unambiguous statement of anything, including the intention of a meaning. (14)

As the young women told these stories of their problematic personal experiences, they gave them multiple meanings. The ways in which the experiences played out, how the young women responded to their situations, and how their families cared, or did not care, affected them deeply. These epiphanic moments (Denzin 1989c) reveal the complex nature of past, present, and hoped-for experiences. Why these young women responded the way they did, placing their energies and focus on education, resulted from many factors, including their families' belief in education and their own desires for betterment. Both the families and the school influenced the ways in which the young women became successful.

The stories focused on how family strengths and experiences in school led these students on a winding path to academic success. This study differs from others in that it shows some of the strengths and success-supporting outcomes of stressed families. The confidence and coherence that Werner and Smith (1982) found in their resilient children resulted from a caring and loving infancy. But this fact could not be confirmed in the five cases I investigated. What I did find was that the extended families, not necessarily the immediate, nuclear families, provided continuing, caring support during the girls' troubled teen years.

The main strength that all the families had was a belief in the value of education (Clark 1983). This belief led them to establish rules, which were often broken, that reinforced the high priority the parents gave to education. Another strength—an outcome of growing up in a stressed family—was that the young women accepted family responsibilities in a mature, adult way. The family circumstances and gender expectations created a mountain of responsibilities that these young women took very seriously.

There was a paradox in the success these young women achieved at school and the stressed lives they led at home. Usually one associates girls' success at school with parents who are interested and participate in their daughters' schooling (Baumrind 1968, 1978). The families in this study, however, did not participate in the outward life of the school yet were characterized by significant protective factors for school success (Clark 1983): they believed in education as a means to success, had an extended family to act as a social safety net, had an eye on the future, and provided certain educational resources, such as a room in which the child could study and be alone. Gender was also found to be a protective factor (Werner and Smith 1982) for academic success because these young women were expected to play an important role in providing for the family, either financially or morally. The strengths, skills, and qualities they developed as a result of these responsibilities were part of the self they brought with them to the school context.

The School

This study extends the work of Garmezy and Rutter (1983) and Werner and Smith (1982) and builds on their findings by providing understandings of the process by which resilient young women succeed at school. What I found in this study confirmed the findings of Garmezy and Rutter (1983) in that three of these young women seized opportunities to take responsibility in school, and this brought them success. They mostly developed warm, supportive relationships with teachers and were planners and organizers. What Garmezy and Rutter did not discover was the way in which these young women negotiate their successes in the school setting. Werner and Smith (1982) found that just attending school enabled some children to be successful. For the young women in this study, not just attending school but also eliciting positive responses from teachers worked to make them successful. But staying away from classes also had a positive effect, enabling these young women to engage in ongoing attempts to organize their fractured experiences. Absence thus acted as a "self-righting mechanism" (Garmezy and Rutter 1983). In itself, absence was not a self-righting mechanism, but what the young women did during their absences relieved the pressure in their lives, enabling them to continue with the pursuit of school success. What they did when absent, besides take part in counseling sessions, was to reflect on their lives, sleep, do homework, care for sick parents, recover from their own illnesses, and visit friends. By being absent often, they were able to lessen the stress in their lives and maintain high standards in their schoolwork. Because they had learned to manipulate the system, their actions incurred no negative consequences.

This study also presents a view of the school, Plains High, including a focus on the diversity of its cultural and social makeup and its success-oriented learning environment. At Plains High, tight discipline and control worked for those who were successful by providing them with a safe environment in which to learn. But it did stifle some of the creativity and spontaneity of its youthful clients. Students who were not successful received fewer benefits from such a tightly disciplined and controlled school.

I showed that at Plains High, academic success was a homogeneous notion. The way to become academically successful was basically the same for all successful students: to get good grades in basically all the same high level classes. What was important to the success of the young women in this study was the way in which they fit into that notion or, at times, got around it. The opportunities to take responsibility in the school and pursue academic studies contributed to the success of these young women (Rutter et al. 1979), as did their getting themselves into advanced classes, having exposure to high-caliber teachers, and soliciting the support of those who knew how to help them get around the system (Powell, Farrar, and Cohen 1985). As well, most of the young women took advantage of a quality counseling program.

Other students, like the dropouts in the comparison study, were unable to manage the stressors in their lives and maintain a good academic record. These five young women were able to manage because of previous experiences of coping under stress, the presence of supportive and protective factors, and their beliefs in a bright future (Benard 1992). They transferred the skills that they learned at home to their schooling and expected to be treated like adults at school. They learned more from teachers who treated them like adults and fought with and stayed away from those who treated them like children. They often complained that the school was not set up as a place where adults gathered—there were uniform rules and regulations for students of all ages, freshmen through seniors.

In chapter 8, "Not Your Usual Success Story," I preempted the possible assertion that these young women were just smart. Yes they were, but no more or less so than others in the comparison groups. I deliberately chose a group of young women with a variety of performance levels as assessed by standardized-test scores. What I found to be key elements of their success were their responsiveness to opportunities offered them at school, which enabled them to be seen as successful, the types of relationships they developed with teachers, particularly female teachers (Davies 1983; Weis 1985a), and that they look forward to a future (Benard 1992). The types of relationships they developed were generally distant. They learned from their families that intimacy has a high price, exacts a time commitment, and can bring distress and destruction. The fact that they didn't develop lasting, intimate relationships with many students at school enabled them to focus on schoolwork. The intimate relationships of students in the comparison group distracted them from their educational pursuits.

The young women realized that by being in the limelight of a leadership position, acting in a play, or holding an official position in a club, they were becoming successful in the eyes of the school. Why these young women were focused on success and why they did what they did were results of a number of interlocking past influences, present supportive experiences, and future aspirations. Most, but not all, had experienced success in elementary school. All spoke of teachers who encouraged and mentored them, who believed in their potential and communicated this to them. They valued these experiences and expectations. Jasmine said that when she "got in with the wrong crowd" in her freshman year, she knew what she was missing when she no longer received encouragement and honors for her work. She missed the respect of teachers and the praise that goes with doing well, so she distanced herself from those friends and went back to concentrating on her schoolwork.

At school, these young women learned what they had to do to become successful. They had to learn what the teachers valued and gain their confidence and respect. They tapped into the caring side of Plains High by using the counseling services, they found teachers who understood their family backgrounds, and they took time out to rest and ease the pressure in their lives. The curriculum of consequence to most of them was the AP and other advanced classes. For Sabrina, the curriculum of consequence was tapping into the personalized attention that the special-education department provided in order to get high grades. Not everyone had that chance; among those who did, not everyone took advantage of the opportunities. The young women in the comparison study took advanced-level classes but did poorly in them compared with the young women in this study who took these classes. They did poorly because they didn't have the same concern for detail or drive for perfection, nor did they have the same sense of coherence and meaning in their lives or the investment in education as a priority. Nor did they have the support and approval of the faculty that these five young women had.

Four of the five young women said they wanted to go to college upon graduation. This fits well with their teachers' expectations of them. The teachers' philosophy of success was defined in terms of going to college. It was exceptional that a student would be given an award for anything other than graduating and planning to go to college.

At the annual Choral Night, the graduating seniors were presented to an audience of parents and community members. They all said they were planning to go to college, a fact contrary to reality. Four of the five young women did in fact enter college after graduating from high school. Only Jasmine completed her degree within four years; the others dropped out or extended their time at college.

The proposal that going on to college is the successful thing to do has a profound influence on what teachers perceive as success and what students think is successful. A few teachers did question the wisdom of this expectation. The music teacher said:

> We act as though we expect all students to go to college. It is a totally unreal- istic expectation. And in fact, what I think we do, sadly, is set kids up for failure. About eighty percent of students go on to some form of further educa- tion, and that sounds impressive, but a lot of them come back. They don't last. They are not exposed to alternatives to college. Most teachers are un- aware of them because we have only been to school ourselves.

The three young women in this study who dropped out of college and those students who were not successful had never been presented with other options. If they could not or would not go to college, they were not acknowledged as successful by their teachers or by the school's administrators.

What some teachers and administrators did for these young women was caringly "get in their faces" to show what was possible; critique their work (Goldenberg 1992), except in Alexis's case; offer opportunities; and push for their continued application. Whereas some young people might reject this attention, these young women demanded it, sought it, and engaged their teachers in a way that made them respond to them. Why were they like that? Because of who they were: their biographies show significant events in their lives that made them strong, demanding people. They set their sights on the future and focused on getting there. The school reacted positively to that sort of focus. Cutting the slack is something Plains High did effectively for these young women. Plains High didn't do it for the majority of students; the number of students with suspensions and detentions points to that fact.

Prescriptions for Success

There are lessons to be learned from the stories of these five young women. Realizing the potential to be an agent in one's own schooling is empowering. Sometimes help may be needed to realize this. If the counseling services at the school are effective, they will assist students in reflecting on how it might be done. Taking care of the stressed self is also important. Time out should be taken to finish schoolwork, rest, and energize oneself so that a focus on educational matters can be a priority. Young people should have their eyes on a goal and realize that education is needed to reach it. Channeling anger and frustration into academic success is one way to remain focused.

In the family, it is important to have a place of one's own, a place to retreat to and rest in. The young women in this study made their rooms their own, with their personal decorations and memorabilia and educational resources. Distancing oneself from family problems is not always possible, but when these problems impinge on educational attainment, the student may need help sorting out priorities. Extended family members are often a source of strength and renewal.

At school, establishing supportive, friendly relationships with teachers who will cut the slack when times are tough is vital. Seizing opportunities that the school offers in order to be seen in a successful role is very important. If students are in prominent positions, they are more likely to feel they have to perform well. This pressure can help if it doesn't become overwhelming. Taking advanced-level classes is also part of being successful. Knowing which teachers are reputable and have a history of success with students is part of the game. So is establishing credit with faculty members so that when time out is needed, it can be taken without retribution. Finding at least one faculty member who is trustworthy and will understand the pressure of a stressed family is important, not only for cutting the slack but in promoting success despite the stressors of life.

There are three main implications for schools. First, the strength of Plains High lay its emphasis on an academic curriculum, which these young women tapped into. The weakness of such an emphasis is that it excludes students who either do not qualify for such a program, or are not aware of its advantages. Addressing the need for the success of the large majority of "unspecial" students is the biggest challenge. The answer to the question of what can be done to promote "success . . . for all" may lie in unpacking the homogeneous notion of academic success that currently exists. This particularly applies to the African American students whom Alexis knew were bright but rejected the curriculum offered at Plains High. Her solution, and perhaps a start, was to provide a more African American-centered curriculum, along with more teachers with an understanding of the issues. In the eyes of the students, these are African American teachers. Models can be seen in some of the Chicago schools that have implemented alternative ways of educating students to build their cultural identity (Madhubuti 1992; Mosely 1992). Ogbu (1991) and Fordham (1988) advocated a curriculum that reflects the organization of the cultural milieu in which students live. Whose knowledge is really valued—that of the teachers or that of the minority groups they teach—needs to be addressed by the faculty.

Using the leadership that already exists in the student body, not as a pacifier of problems but as an empowering means to promote cooperation between the administration and the school, is also something to be considered. Capitalizing on the political orientation of the African American students rather than ignoring or respectfully tolerating differences is the key to success for these students. More support of what these students value, such as interests showcased in the African American Talent Show, is needed. The racial tensions that shaped the beginnings of Plains High have not been fully resolved. As the statistics indicate, they will go on well into the next century, only changing in complexity. Solutions, such as the provision of the special programs that were worked out twenty years ago, need to be redefined; there are other solutions these days (McCarthy 1993; Peshkin 1992). Ignoring the challenges of differences only fuels unrest. Alexis spent a lot of her time at Plains High addressing race issues so that they would not be ignored. With groups of African American students and with white students she stressed tolerance and understanding. Not all the African American students wanted to be, or could have been, successful the way Alexis was. The tensions of her finding a voice within the school drove her to want to find a space at Plains High. She found it in trying to reconcile the diverse interests of some African American students and the school. Many of the other African American students rejected schooling altogether. But because she had experienced success and recognition at school, she wanted that experience for others.

The second implication for schools is the young women's use of absenteeism for recuperation. There is no doubt that if they had attended school more often, they would have done better academically. But that is not the point. They did not attend school regularly, and I believe this was to relieve the stress in their lives. Attending a counseling session or taking time for themselves was important to their later success.

If a culture of respect truly exists, then young people of seventeen, eighteen, or nineteen should be able to decide for themselves when they need to take time off. Having the same disciplinary regulations for students in all grades doesn't help in creating an environment of trust and autonomy for the juniors and seniors. Opportunities for students to act as agents in their own success need to be built into the thinking of teachers and administrators, and these opportunities should not be just for those who have acquired idiosyncratic credit but also for the "unspecial" students (Powell, Farrar, and Cohen 1985).

The third implication is the use of counseling within the school for stressed students. This was a major factor not only in the emotional balance of the students in this study but also in their academic success at school. It enabled them to defuse totally distracting situations. As Jasmine said, "If I didn't have it [counseling], I would have just blown up in class." The close connection between the use of counseling and the young women's academic success was not always seen by the faculty. Teachers complained that students missed too many classes because of counseling, and students were expected to make up the extra work they'd missed. If the faculty had realized the importance of counseling in many of these young women's lives, they might not have seen classroom attendance as the most important factor in success. As one teacher admitted, she was willing to make adjustments, but unless a student told her that she was at counseling, she would not know to make the adjustments.

Confidentiality between the counseling staff and its clients is very important. Yet the tensions created because the teachers are kept in the dark in regard to their students' should be discussed by the faculty, and some policy regarding shared information should be developed.

End Thoughts

There is something worth learning from the stories of how these young women found their way to success in a public high school—lessons for teachers, administrators, counselors, and most important, other young people who "suffer the slings and arrows of outrageous fortune." A homogeneous notion of success in education masks the potential that lies in every school. A focus not on the deficits of youths who come from stressed families but on their strengths (Weick 1992) provides different insights into pathways these young people might take. A focus on strengths includes the strengths of schools and how they might be expanded to include more students within the ranks of the successful. Schools should not only teach about diversity (Peshkin 1992); they should also provide diverse opportunities for students to be successful. To redefine notions of success and back them up with resources that only a small percentage of students currently enjoy would be to "boldly pursue success and excellence for all."

Methodological Appendix

This appendix describes the research methods used to understand how young women with multiple stressors achieved school success. There were many stories heard along the way that I chose not to tell, and there were many more that I did not hear as I walked the hallways of the school, sat in living rooms of homes, and drove to cafés with the young women. This is not a study of how *all* young women at Plains High achieved success, nor is it an evaluation of Plains High's success rate with young women. It is not a prediction of what these five young women will do or become in the future. It is a study of how a particular group of young women, a group with multiple stressors in their lives, were successful at school. The narratives told here crisscross the landscapes of school and home, showing what life was like for these young women on the road to academic success. The purpose of the study was to understand in some way what these young women did that made them successful and what contextual factors supported them in their bid for academic success. I wanted to understand how they kept their sights on success despite the many stressors in their lives.

First, I explain why qualitative research methods were chosen for this study. Second, I place the research methods within the context of other educational research in this field. Third, I explain the permissions and access negotiated for this project. Fourth, I describe the methods I used. Fifth, I set out the process of coding, analysis, and writing.

Qualitative Research—Naturalistic Inquiry

One of the purposes of qualitative research is to understand the experience of people, usually from their own perspective. Different theories underpin the use of qualitative research, and while their list is not exhaustive, Bogdan and Biklen (1992) have identified the five most commonly used paradigms: phenomenology, symbolic interaction, cultural theory, ethnomethodology, and cultural studies. I did not align myself exclusively with any one of these paradigms, but I did draw extensively from all of them.

From phenomenology, I attempted to understand the meaning of events from the perspective of the participant. I am particularly aware of the fact that subjectivity plays an important part in the choice of topic to study, the way in which the question is studied, and the way in which the results are interpreted (Peshkin 1985, 1988, 1992).

Meaning is conferred by teachers, parents, and friends. From symbolic interaction I widened my search for meaning to others in order to better interpret what I was seeing. From symbolic interaction, I also took the concept of self as seeing oneself as others see one (Denzin 1989a; Erickson 1986).

From cultural theory, I used the notion of description: to make known what is only partially understood by the participants and the audience. Thick description gives the reader an experience of what it is like on the "inside" (Geertz 1973; Wax, 1971).

From ethnomethodology, I understood and used the language that the participants used to reveal the layers of local meanings and understandings (West and Zimmerman 1987).

Cultural studies placed the study theoretically in the language of feminism, emphasizing the intersection of social structure and human agency (Benhabib 1992; Roman and Apple 1990).

The Context of Research in Education

The educational rationale for this study comes from the fact that many theories of educational success and failure separate personal factors (attribution or expectancy theory and cognitive schema theory), family factors (Clark 1983), school factors (the effective-schools literature), and community factors (community psychology; the critical cultural theorists, such as Weis 1985a, 1985b, 1990). The separation of these factors precludes the study of self, family, school, and community as a holistic dynamic process. Recently, there have been moves to bring a more holistic approach to the study of success and failure. Weis (1990) explained school achievement in the light of current social movements. But she admitted that more work needs to be done on understanding the place of family in the process: "Families are still, however, one of the least researched institutions of society. This is undoubtedly the case because families are still considered 'private.' It is still much easier, for example, to gain access to a school than a family for participant-observation work" (227).

Benard (1992), who has drawn together much of the literature on protective factors within the family, school, and community, quoted Werner as saying: "Data analysis that explores the interplay among multiple risks and protective factors at all three levels—the individual, the immediate family, and the larger social context—are still rare" (5).

Phelan, Davidson, and Cao (1991) described the interrelationships between family, school, and peers and examined the perceptions of boundary crossing between these contexts:

> Thus far, there has been almost no attempt to understand how students' multiple worlds interact with one another, or the process young people use to manage, more or less successfully, the transitions between various social settings. Steinberg (1988, 43) also notes this neglect in educational research: "Virtually absent from the literature are studies that examine students, and contextual influences in interaction with each other." (226)

This is the point at which this study begins. The call to integrate the personal with the public in the matter of being educated has its roots in Mills's (1959) exhortation that we must learn to use our life experiences in our intellectual work and that public issues or troubles should be developed in research by relating them to personal struggles. I integrate the self-as-agent with family and school and community agency in order to shed light on what the girls brought from one setting to another in order to be successful at school. How they negotiated their ways through both failure and success to be perceived as successful people is what is being unwrapped.

Much of the literature on school success has focused on the strengths of the individual, family, school, or community. In this study of successful young women, I found that the young women's lives were fraught with problems at home and at school, and I found a society that was not always kind to them or their families. Yet somehow they managed to struggle through the mess, seize on the strengths that were inherent in each of the settings, negotiate failures, and find opportunities to become successful at school. With regard to where resilient students find support, Benard (1991) said:

> If a child's major risks lie in the family system, such as growing up in an alcoholic, abusive, or schizophrenic home, many of the factors identified as protective will derive from the school or community environments. Likewise, when a child's major risks come from the community system, usually the

condition of living in poverty—as over one-fourth of the children in the United States now do—protective factor research has usually examined the role that the family and school systems play in the development of resiliency. (5)

Rather than designating one system—for example, the family—as an at-risk element in a student's life, I preferred to look for strengths and weaknesses across settings, to discover how students use strengths and perceive failure across contexts. Benard (1992) alluded to the value of such an approach: "Of course, given the self-righting nature of human systems, researchers have also identified strengths and protective attributes even within environments characterized overall by great risks. Unfortunately . . . most studies of vulnerable children have defined risk at only one level of organization" (5).

Csikszentmihalyi and Larson (1984) identified another problem in researching young people. They said that it is easier to document students' progress in school, changes in behavior, or other factors influencing teenage development than it is to document what they called the "subjective" experiences of the adolescent.

The fluidity of adolescence allows freedom to alter the course of life, but it does make the job of social scientists a great deal harder. Psychologists like to be able to explain what people have done and to predict what they will be doing. Confronted with the provocative contradictions of this age, they are likely to be frustrated. (xiii)

This study looks at the difficult subjective experiences of five adolescent women as they move from home to school. It moves across those contextual boundaries that the literature refers to.

Permissions and Access

The Permissions
Getting permission and gaining access to a site are not one unified process. Permission is getting approval to be on a research site—for example, a school. Access is the path taken once inside the door. The more complicated elements of access are gaining the trust and confidence of students and faculty members so that they can feel comfortable in the researcher's presence and are willing to share that part of their lives that speak to the study. Gaining both permission and access involves considerable time and energy (Weade 1990).

To get permission to conduct this study at Plains High, I first asked the principal, but I also wanted the faculty members to have a say, so

I wrote to them and broadly set out the proposed study. My request went through the school advisory committee and then on to the various departmental meetings. I also attended a meeting of the Advisory Committee to speak about the proposal. All levels within the school agreed to the research. Once local permission was obtained, the official permission through the school district was easy to secure. The application to do research in the school was sent to the school district through the University of Illinois. The school district sent the application to the principal, and he approved it.

Before entering into the formal, focused part of this research, I spent a year on a field project at Plains High. When I entered the school in August 1990, I knew no one, and no one knew me. It did not take long before some staff members took pity on me and invited me to sit in on their classes. This gave me a feel for the atmosphere and the ambience of the school. This contact placed me firmly in the school as a researcher. It also gave me time to locate possible participants for the project. This was the beginning of the cordial relationship that enabled me to ask to return to do my research. Negotiating with the multiple gatekeepers in a school is an ongoing task:

> The keys to access are almost always in the hands of multiple gatekeepers, both formal and informal. In most cases those gatekeepers, before giving assent, will want to assess the costs and the risks that it will pose, both for themselves and for the groups to which they control access. (Lincoln and Guba 1985, 253)

During the course of the research, I was continually negotiating access with teachers as they became involved in the project. Gaining access is something that is imbedded in the ongoing context of ethnographic research.

Contacting the Respondents

Making a final decision about whom to include in the study took place over three stages. In the semester before I decided on the five young women to be part of this study, I asked teachers to recommend girls who might like to talk with me about "how and why young women succeed at school." I added that I particularly wanted to speak with young women who they knew had significant stress in their lives and yet had done well at school. Several teachers gave me names, as did some of the counselors. One dean listed all the students in the Upward Bound Program, an organization for African American students who were doing well at school and were from low-income families or families on welfare.

Individually and in groups, I told these girls about my study and asked them whether they would like to do an initial interview with me. In this initial interview, I wanted to establish whether or not they were open and willing to talk, had circumstances in their lives that caused them stress, were prepared to introduce me to their families and friends, and were on the school honor roll—my only external indicator of academic success at that early stage.

All thirty girls I talked to were very interested in the topic and wanted to be part of the project, so I conducted the first interview with all of them. I sent a letter to their parents, asking permission for their daughters to be part of the project. Many parents commented that they were pleased with my study. Later several of the girls looked out for me at school and introduced me to their friends. Some gave me their writing to read and generally indicated that they were delighted to be listened to. One girl introduced me to her mother, and several others asked me to sit in on classes whose teachers they thought were "good." I had a mailbox in the main office and told the girls that contact could be made by leaving me a note there. I gave the girls my home phone number so they could call me if they wanted to.

I did not want a homogeneous group of young women as respondents for this project. A homogeneous group may produce findings that appear to be generalizable; with a diverse group, that tendency is reduced. I wanted as diverse a group as possible: diverse in ethnic background, IQ ratings, and the types of problems encountered in being successful. In order to achieve this, I decided to ask the girls to recommend other girls they knew who they thought would be suitable. I thought that they might know more details about the home lives of their friends than some of the teachers did. This proved to be true. I made contact with another ten to fifteen girls this way, and I decided to shadow three of them to get a feel for their daily lives. *Shadowing*, a term used in qualitative research, means spending time with, following, or observing. Shadowing gave me insights into the daily flow of life at the school and indicated some of the areas I needed to know more about when it came to constructing my interview schedules.

From the forty-five young women I initially interviewed, I chose five for the project. I chose these five because teachers and students had recommended them to me as successful—all but one had a GPA of 4.5

or above; they indicated to me that they had significant stressors in their lives; they were willing to be part of the project; and they were articulate about themselves and their experiences. I told them that I was going to write a book that would explain what I found out about the topic. I gave each of them the transcript of the interview so that they could read it and so that we could talk about the issues I saw arising from the interview. To give a summary of my reasons for choosing these young women, I outline in table form the indicators of success (Table 3) and stress (Table 4) that I found among these young women.

The intelligence factor. While the stories show the many influences on these young women, readers might infer that these girls were successful because of their superior intelligence. What part did being "intelligent" or "just smart" play in their achieving success despite the odds being against it? Their standardized-test results ranged from high to low. In year eleven (junior year), their aptitude scores, general composite scores with 100 as the mean, were as follows: Jackie, 126; Alexis, 111; Sabrina, 98; Jasmine, 136; Xia, 141. Cultural factors may have lowered Jasmine's and Alexis's scores. Given the range, one might conclude that intelligence may have been influential with Jackie, Jasmine, and Xia. But Alexis and Sabrina were successful, too, even with average standardized-test scores. At the beginning of this study, before I made a final decision about whom to include, I found several young women whose standardized-test scores were as high as those of the girls I eventually chose and who had family stress but either did not do well at school or dropped out. High test results were not a consistent predictor of success in this study; success was more complex.

For example, Xia consistently scored in the ninety-ninth percentile on verbal and mathematical skills. One could argue that she was able to write good essays because she was smart. Her peers in class admired her smartness and said they wished they could think like her. Most of the intellectual discussions that Xia initiated in class seemed to reflect the types of discussions she had with her friends outside of school, in the coffee shops on the local college campus. She didn't seem to have to spend too much time doing assignments; her problem was making time to get the assignments done. Her success was partly being seen by her peers and her teachers as a result of her being smart; because she was perceived as smart, she was elected to direct

Table 3 Respondent Profiles—Successes

Respondent	GPA	Recommended by Teacher	Recommended by Peer	Office-holder	Involved in Extra-curricular Activities	Leader	Out-of-School Leader	Recipient of Prizes or Awards	Enrolled in AP Classes
Jackie	4.621	x	x					x	x
Alexis	3.900	x	x	x	x	x	x	x	
Sabrina	4.625	x	x					x	
Jasmine	4.666	x	x	x	x	x		x	x
Xia	4.571	x	x	x	x	x	x	x	x

x positive response

Table 4 Respondent Profiles—Stressors

Respondent	Marital Discord/ Divorce	Alcohol/ Drug Abuse	Low SES/ Poverty	Sexual/ Physical Abuse	Suicide Attempt	Anorexia	Depression	Criminal History	After School Job
Jackie		x (f)r,t	x (f)r,t,o				x (f,r)t,o		x (r)r,t,o
Alexis	x (md)t	x (f)t		x (r,pa)r	x (r)r		x (r)r,t,o	x (f)r	
Sabrina	x (md)r,t,o	x (f)r,t	x (f)r,t	x (r,pa)r,t	x (f)		x (r)r,o		x (r)r
Jasmine	x (d)r	x (r)r,t	x (f)r,o	x (r,sa,pa)r,t	x (r)r,t,o	x (r)r	x (r)r,t,o	x (r)r	
Xia	x (d)r,t	x (f)r	x (f)r,t	x (r,pa)	x (f)r		x (r)r,t,o	x (f)r	x (r)r,t,o

x   Stressor is present
(r)   Stressor applies to respondent
(f)   Stressor applies to family member(s)
(md)   Marital discord in family
(d)   Divorce of respondent's parents
(pa)   Physical abuse of respondent
(sa)   Sexual abuse of respondent
r   Knowledge gained from an interview with the respondent
t   Knowledge gained from an interview with a teacher
o   Knowledge gained from observation

several class projects. This turned out to be a two-edged sword: she was so often absent that the other students became frustrated when she was not there to lead them or when they couldn't work because she had taken some essential materials home.

Sabrina, at the other end of the scale, scored in the second to fourth percentile on verbal and math skills. One could argue that she needed special-education services just to complete her work. But by the time she entered her senior year, she was no longer under the auspices of the special-education department. She was motivated enough and knowledgeable enough about how to complete assignments that she no longer needed those services. The level at which she became independent was at the basic level of performance. Sabrina overcame the odds of ill health and family stress and was perceived by teachers and peers as a very successful student.

The young women in this study were unaware of, or had forgotten, their test scores, and overall the scores didn't seem to play a large role in their perception of their achievements. When asked why they were successful, they never mentioned intelligence. Being perceived as smart by teachers and students was probably more influential. Several students in the comparison study had high test scores but poor academic records. Equally intelligent but negatively viewed students sometimes were not academically successful.

The comparison studies. In order to highlight what made these young women different from other students with similar successes and stresses, I did three small comparison studies.

The first group I interviewed comprised three young women who teachers thought should have done well but did not. They scored high on standardized tests, but their grades were Cs, Ds, and Fs. These young women also had significant stressors in their private lives. I wanted to find out why they did not do well and compare them with the five young women in this study. The second group were the top five female graduates of the class of 1992. I sent each of them a survey, asking them to explain why they thought they were successful and to what they attributed their success. I then interviewed the two who returned the survey, one of whom was the school valedictorian. Again I wanted to know the differences, if any, between these young women and those on whom this study focused. The third group consisted of two young women who had GPAs over 4.0, high standardized-test scores, and multiple stressors in their lives and eventually dropped out of school. One of these young women had a baby; the other did not.

I controlled the selection of participants in the comparison studies for these factors: high GPAs, high standardized-test scores, and significant stressors. I conducted two to three interviews with each of these young women and sat in on some of their classes. I did these small comparison studies to see what I might learn from them that would highlight differences between them and the successful young women of this study.

Methods

The most commonly used methods of qualitative research are participant observation, interviewing, and document analysis. I used all three in my study. Denzin (1989a) said that gaining knowledge by different methods is a form of triangulation, a form of rigor applied to understanding empirical situations.

Observation

Before beginning formal interviews, I spent one year at the school making observations. During the first semester, I was at the school two full days a week and often in the evenings, and on weekends for extracurricular activities. During the second semester, I was at the school three full days a week and for after-school activities. The two semesters I spent in the school placed me as a learner (Glesne and Peshkin 1992) observing the life of the school: "It is important to recognize that a great deal of what is important to observe is unspoken" (Whyte and Whyte 1984, 83). Because I went to my research site as a learner, I did not presume to know the answers to the questions I was asking. I put myself in different situations where I could observe, think, and seek the connections between the parts of what it was I was exploring—resilience, gender, and success.

Gold (1958) said that there are four types of participant-observer roles, ranging from the complete observer to the complete participant. I prefer to think of this distinction between participant and observer as a continuum along which we are constantly moving, rather than as four types. One is not either participant or observer. My being an observer in a classroom, for example, was problematic because my presence had an effect on the teacher and, sometimes, on the students. It could be dramatic—as it sometimes was on the first visit—or less intrusive, as it could be on subsequent visits to the same class-room. During the first visit to a classroom, it was important to inform the teacher that I was not there as an evaluator of the class nor as a co-teacher but to observe the young women in the class. (It was only toward the end of my fieldwork that some teachers were aware of who the participants in the study were.) The teachers were aware of my presence and, to differing degrees, made adjustments. I asked the young women whether the teachers acted differently when I was present. They told me that generally they were much the same as always. I found that returning to a class several times put the teacher more at ease and that behaviors that were a result of having a researcher in the classroom gradually diminished. "The naturalness of the observer role, coupled with its nondirection, makes it the least noticeably instrusive of all research techniques" (Phillips, quoted in Adler and Adler 1994, 382).

Bogdan and Biklen (1992) encouraged the close connection be-tween observation and data collection but pointed out that we cannot always be in a position to collect data and might have to do some "rapport building" (90), which results in better data collection at a later date. I do not see the distinction between moments of "rapport" and "data collection." The fusing of presences is part of the immer-sion process that is required for collaborative research such as this. Only in retrospect did I realize that some instances of observation might have been labeled more productive for data collection than others.

Because the possibility of discovery had to be maximized (Becker and Geer 1982) I enhanced my observations, often using Spradley's (1980) nine dimensions: attending to the use of space, the actors, the activities, the physical objects present (as distinct from the people), the actions of those present, the event taking place, the time sequence, the goals of the activity, and the feelings and emotions generated by the activity. I would later frame my diary entries according to these helpful categories.

Observations were not always confined to classrooms. I often walked the hallways during the day to get a sense of the school at work. I read bulletinboards, and I listened to announcements. I heard the language that was used by the students and the teachers. I was aware that it was different from my language, not only because I am Australian but also because most of the speakers—the students—were young people. I tried to understand the way they talked about the school and their lives. I attended extracurricular functions, including a homecoming dance, a prom, basketball games, before-school band practice, and after-school club meetings. I saw some teachers who spent long hours at the school, coming in at 7:00 A.M. for meetings and staying after school for other meetings, which often lasted until 10:00 P.M. All this gave me a sense of the school beyond the fifty-minute, seven-period day.

Observation is being aware of as many aspects of life as possible. I observed the girls in their homes, in fast-food stores, and in places of work, usually while I was conducting interviews with them. In some homes, I was invited back on a social basis. Jackie, after reading her story, humorously commented, "Wow, I knew you were watching, but not this closely." I took that as a compliment.

Refusals were a part of this research, too. I never met Sabrina's parents; she did not want me to meet them. Even though I asked several times and told her why I needed to talk with them, she refused because she believed her parents "would not tell the truth. They would put on a false face." I respected this decision eventually and saw it as a limitation of this study. I also saw that my respect for her feelings must be part of the method and so I did not go against her wishes. I tried to make up for this limitation by gathering as much information about her parents from teachers who knew her family situation. Alexis's parents gave permission for their daughter to participate in the study but did not want to be interviewed themselves. I visited her home on various occasions and spoke with her father informally. With the other three young women, I was fortunate to meet and interview the parents and, sometimes, the grandparents, brothers and sisters, and other relatives.

Interviewing

I believed that these interviews should be like conversations (Jansen 1992) so that students might bring up issues that I might have thought of as irrelevant but on reflection would realize brought new ideas and connections to my topic. But Glesne and Peshkin (1992) gave a realistic reminder: "By whatever means obtained, the questions you ask must fit your topic: the answers they elicit must illuminate the phenomenon of inquiry. And the questions you ask must be anchored in the cultural reality of your respondents: the questions must be drawn from the respondents' lives" (66).

During the interviews, I tried not to listen just to the respondents' words. I looked for body language that showed signs of stress, anxiety, happiness, or sadness and noted this in the field notes that I wrote up each evening. I formally interviewed each young woman approximately ten times. I taped half these interviews and took notes during the others. I taped at least one formal interview with the parents and other relatives, and I taped thirty interviews with teachers, each lasting from thirty to fifty minutes. The taped interviews were then transcribed. I took notes during other interviews I conducted with family members and teachers.

For the interviews I conducted at the school, I usually used the small office that I was assigned for the duration of my study. It was in the student-services area, and when I was not there, it was used as a holding room for detained students. It also housed information and handbooks from colleges around the United States. It measured four feet by six and contained a desk, two chairs, one full-length bookcase, and a file cabinet. There was little room in which to move about, and interviewing, at first seemed cramped. After our first few interviews, the young women and I became accustomed to the closeness of the room. When the weather was fine, we occasionally sat outside. I also found public holidays and weekends excellent opportunities for the long interviews (one and a half to two and a half hours) that were not possible during the forty-five to fifty-minute period slots at school. Teachers preferred to be interviewed in their own classrooms or in the hallways while they were on hall duty.

I took the approach of developing a close relationship with those I interviewed, thus minimizing the difference between the interviewee and the interviewer (Fontana and Frey 1994). Because I was a guest in the school and teachers knew that I was there on their conditions, I felt that the power differential was weighted toward the teachers. I had also given them assurances that they would have an opportunity to read and critique the final document. They, of course, may have felt that I was the one with power because I had control over the final document. These tensions are a healthy part of the process of reflecting on collection of data, and while awareness of these issues does not mean that they were resolved, it does suggest that the requisite openness and honesty between partners were present, and this could only have helped to make the process as transparent as possible.

Document Analysis

I had access to two sorts of documents. The first were the school files on the young women and the second were personal diaries and essays that the young women wrote.

I read the young women's cumulative files, which contained academic and personal records from middle school through high school. These are available to teachers and do not contain confidential information. Nonetheless, I sought permission from the young women and the school administration before I read them. From these files, I obtained semester grades, GPAs, standardized-test results, and an accounting of the school activities the young women were involved in. I compared my findings from these files with the young women during our interviews.

Allport (quoted in Bogdan and Biklen 1992) said that "the spontaneous and intimate diary is the personal document par excellence," (133). Van Manen (1990) said that the diary helps people reflect on significant aspects of their life. I asked each of the young women to keep a dairy for me in the last few months of the school year and to write in it about their school experiences and what they thought had made them successful. I collected these works a few times during the course of those months and again one month after the end of the year. These very personal diaries gave me insights into the joys and anxieties that the girls experienced but did not always get time to talk about in our interviews. Toward the end of the school year, I asked them to reflect in their diaries on their involvement in this project.

Several of the young women also showed me autobiographical works they had written as class assignments, usually in their freshman year. These were rich sources of history and family activities. Old photographs gave the young women an opportunity to explain their family histories to me.

Lastly, I read essays and poems by the young women on various topics, including the American hero, black-on-black violence, and other issues of social concern. Document analysis can take many forms and constitutes data that were not obtained in interviews or by observation.

Reciprocity

With the young women who took part in this project, I developed a relationship of friendship. I offered them a genuine interest in their lives, which they accepted. From time to time, I took them to lunch. The school had an open-lunch policy and so we drove to a local fast-food outlet, either in their cars or in mine. On occasion, I was able to help out in some small way, but the best indicator that the young women were getting something out of this project came when, at the end of the debriefing session, after they had read the stories, I asked them whether they would be interested in being part of a longitudinal study. All of them said they would be very happy to continue the project over a longer period of time. They felt that they enjoyed being part of the study. Rossman (1984) believes that reciprocity is an ambiguous concept. She said that it means "exchange," where two people give and take something. Reciprocity can take the form of nontangible rewards that the researcher is giving in return for shared perceptions. The sharing is more symbolic than substantive.

Record Keeping

> A significant attribute of writing is the ability to communicate not only with others but with oneself. A permanent record enables one to reread as well as record one's own thoughts and jottings. In this way one can review and reorganize one's own work, reclassify what one has already classified, rearrange works, sentences, and paragraphs in a variety of ways. . . . The way that information is organized as it is recopied gives us an invaluable insight into the workings of the mind. (Jack Goody, cited in Sanjek 1990, 1)

I kept several types of written records. The first was my *notebook*. I carried this notebook with me everywhere. In it, I recorded my daily timetable, the meetings and interviews I had during the day, and my plans for future visits to the school. I also took notes in it while in classes and during interviews, and at night I referred to it when I wrote up my formal *log*. The formal log contained my reflections on the day in the field and my subjective reactions to situations I encountered. I wrote on only one side of the page, then reread what I had written and made comments alongside it. I also recorded summaries of readings, and quotes that I thought I'd use later. I subscribed to the local newspaper so that I could keep in touch with the public image of the school and read other newspapers for comments on education in general. I had a *filing system* of manila folders, each of which had a heading. In these, I kept articles or summaries of articles on cards. I also had a *theme book*. In this, I had a page for each theme relating to this study, no matter how small it was. Under each theme, I subcoded things that happened in the field and that were likely to build up into a paragraph or an idea for the later writing stage.

Coding, Analysis, and Writing

I decided to write the young women's stories first, as this seemed to me to be the most challenging part of my written work. I divided all my notes and interview transcripts into seven files, one for each of the five young women, one on the school, and one on myself as a researcher. As I read through them, I became aware of the connections between biography and schooling. Each of the young women had unique strengths and stressors in her life at home and at school. As I read the transcripts of interviews and my notes, I looked for categories and asked myself, "What is this an example of?" I then tried to define what I meant by that category, and I looked for evidence of its existence in other places. As I formed a category, I made a file for it in which I placed articles and notes. I became committed to coding as the project progressed. This gave me time to think over sections of transcripts or notes and go back into the field the next day or the next week and pick up where I had left off.

As I read the material again and again, I found that these young women were agents of their own success. This led to the development of the notion of the self-as-agent. But the contexts in which the girls operated were also very important in molding and fashioning their behavior. The complex and contradictory nature of the stories led me to create many categories for coding. At one time, I had over ninety-five categories, or reasons why I thought these young women were successful. The reduction of these categories into groups and subgroups took time and much thinking. I informed my analysis in several ways: I read more literature on success and achievement, I read about dropouts, and I discussed my findings with a group of professional peers who met every week during the spring and summer to discuss methodological and theoretical aspects of our research projects. These "disinterested peers" (Lincoln and Guba 1985, 308) helped keep me honest, squashed some of my wilder notions, and provided the forum for the airing of all that pent-up data. And most important of all, I took the ideas I consolidated in this group back to the young women to see whether they made sense to them. After they had read sections of the transcript, I would ask them, "Do I get it?" meaning "Have I captured your story of success at school according to how you see things?" I was always pleased when they nodded and agreed or when they wanted to make changes here and there to better capture an intended meaning or even to correct factual inaccuracies. Through this checking process, I validated my text (Lincoln and Guba 1985). Two of the young women commented that it was like reading about someone else and having the feeling that "Yes, I can relate to that!" In the end, I decided to form three major headings under which the data would be organized: the self, the family, and the school. These were interactive categories, places of acting and being acted upon.

Glesne and Peshkin (1992) said that the writer has several roles: artist, translator-interpreter, and transformer. The artist seeks "imaginative connections" (153) among the data. Sound links are those that have been found perhaps in more than one place, that have come from different sources. Some call this triangulation; others, trustworthiness. There is a mixture of "gravity and creativity" (152) in the creation of text: gravity, when the issues are serious and one is attempting to represent an experience in as faithful a manner as possible; creativity, when one calls upon various sources to strengthen and enlighten the meaning.

The translator-interpreter role comes with seeing some old situations with new eyes. As translator and interpreter of a culture, I had to present to the reader a sense of the lives of the young women I studied, a sense of how they became successful at school and how they lived their lives through crises and good times. There were many "*I*'s" that I used when I came to interpreting what I had heard and seen (Peshkin 1992). There was the subjective *I*, which saw what I saw through my own experience. There was the interpretive *I*, through which I interpreted what I'd heard and seen through the theoretical discourses that I read.

The transformer role can offer readers insights into old problems. Not every book affects the educational world in such a way that big transformations occur. But every qualitative researcher affects those studied and, most of all, oneself. What I learned from being in the lives of others told me a lot about myself. Schweder (cited in Glesne and Peshkin 1992) said:

> Good ethnography is an intellectual exorcism in which, forced to take the perspective of the other, we are wrenched out of our self. We transcend ourselves, and for a brief moment we wonder who we are, whether we are animals, barbarians or angels, whether all things are really the same under the sun, whether it would be better if the other were us, or better if we were the other. (155)

Schweder also said that "culture is never reducible to what meets the eye, and you can't get ethnographic reality by just looking. . . . If it is real at all, you can only know it by inference and conjecture" (153). Apted (1992), in speaking about his series of films, starting with *7 Up* and ending with *35 Up,* said that "truth is more extraordinary than fiction. That is, real-life stories can be more unbelievable, more daring, and more vivid than invention" (11). The choice of qualitative research methods allowed me to bring that experience to the text, recreating the ways in which these young women became successful.

References

Adler, P. A., and P. Adler. 1994. Observational techniques. In *Handbook of qualitative research*, eds. N. K. Denzin and Y. S. Lincoln, 377–93. Newbury Park, Calif.: Sage.

Apted, M. 1992. Filming life, he found his own. *New York Times*, January 12.

Aptheker, B. 1989. *Tapestries of life: Women's work, women's consciousness, and the meaning of daily experience*. Amherst, Mass.: University of Massachusetts Press.

Bandura, A. 1977. Self-efficacy: Toward a unifying theory of behavioral change. *Psychological Review* 84:191–215.

Bandura, A., and D. H. Schunk. 1981. Cultivating competence, self-efficacy, and intrinsic interest through proximal self-motivation. *Journal of Personality and Social Psychology* 41:586–98.

Baumrind, D. 1968. Authoritarian vs. authoritative parental control. *Adolescence* 3:253–72.

———. 1978. Parental disciplinary patterns and social competence in children. *Youth and Society* 9:239–76.

Beasley, P. L. 1988. The relationship between students' views about the purpose of school and their race, socio-economic status, educational aspiration, and academic self-concept. Ph.D. diss. University of Tennessee, 1988. Abstract in *Dissertation Abstracts International* 50:03A.

Becker, R. G., and B. Geer. 1982. Participant observation: The analysis of qualitative field data. In *Field research*, ed. R. G. Burgess, 239–50. Sydney: George Allen and Unwin.

Benard, B. 1987. *Protective factor research: What we can learn from resilient children.* Calif.: AHTDS Prevention Resource Center.

———. 1991. *Fostering resiliency in kids: Protective factors in the family, school, and community.* Portland, Ore.: North Western Regional Center for Drug-Free Schools and Communities.

———. 1992. Fostering resiliency in kids: Protective factors in the family, school, and community. *Prevention Forum* 12:1–16.

———. 1995. Fostering resilience in children. *ERIC Digest* EDO-PS-95-9.

Benhabib, S. 1992. *Situating the self: Gender, community, and postmodernism in contemporary ethics.* New York: Routledge.

Benson, C. S., and K. Heller. 1987. Factors in the current adjustment of young adult daughters of alcoholic and problem drinking fathers. *Journal of Abnormal Psychology* 96:305–12.

Bergquist, D. K., S. B. Borgers, and N. Tollefson. 1985. *Women's attitudes and educational aspirations.* Lawrence: University of Kansas. Technical Document 143. ERIC, ED 277 904.

Berliner, B., and B. Benard. 1995. How schools can foster resilience in children. NWREL *Western Center News* (September).

Betz, N. E., and L. F. Fitzgerald. 1987. *The career psychology of women.* Orlando, Fla.: Academic Press.

Bogdan, R. C., and S. K. Biklen. 1992. *Qualitative research for education: An introduction to theory and methods.* Boston: Allyn and Bacon.

Callahan, C. M. 1991. An update on gifted females. *Journal for the Education of the Gifted* 14:284–31.

Callan, S. F. 1988. *To drop out or not: At-risk students' perspectives and experiences.* Ph.D. diss. Harvard University, Cambridge.

Cameron-Bandler, L. 1986. Strategies for creating a compelling future. *Focus on Family and Chemical Dependency* (July/August): 6–7, 37, 44.

Clark, R. M. 1983. *Family life and school achievement: Why poor black children succeed or fail.* Chicago: University of Chicago Press.

Cohen, J. 1996. *Girls in the middle: Working to succeed in school.* Washington, D.C.: American Association of University Women Educational Foundation.

Connell, R. W. 1985. *Teacher's work.* Sydney: George Allen and Unwin.

Connell, R. W., D. J. Ashenden, S. Kessler, and G. W. Dowsett. 1982. *Making the difference: Schools, families, and social division.* Sydney: George Allen and Unwin.

Corner, J. P. 1988. Teaching social skills to at-risk children. *Education Week* (November 30): 28.

Csikszentmihalyi, M., and R. Larson. 1984. *Being adolescent: Conflict and growth in the teenage years.* New York: Basic Books.

Danziger, S. K., and N. B. Farber. 1990. Keeping inner-city youths in schools: Critical experiences of young black women. *Social Work* 26, no. 4:32–39.

Davies, L. 1983. Gender, resistance, and power. In *Gender, class, and education,* eds. S. Walker and L. Barton, 39–52. Barcombe, England: Falmer Press.

Denzin, N. K. 1989a. *The research act: A theoretical introduction to sociological methods.* 3rd ed. Englewood Cliffs, N.J.: Prentice-Hall.

———. 1989b. *Interpretive biography.* Newbury Park, Calif.: Sage.

———. 1989c. *Interpretive Interactionism.* Newbury Park, Calif.: Sage.

Dweck, C. 1975. The role of expectations and attributions in the alleviation of learned helplessness. *Journal of Personality and Social Psychology* 31:674–85.

Eisner, E. W. 1979. *The educational imagination.* New York: Macmillan.

Erickson, F. 1986. Qualitative methods in research on teaching. In *Handbook of research on teaching.* 3rd ed, ed. M. C. Wittrock, 119–61. New York: Macmillan.

Farmer, H. 1977. What inhibits achievement and career motivation in women? In *Counseling women,* eds. L. Harmon, L. Fitzgerald, J. Birk, and M. Tanney, 159–72. Monterey, Calif.: Brooks/Cole.

———. 1985. Model of career and achievement motivation for women and men. *Journal of Counseling Psychology* 32:363–90.

Fennema, E., and J. A. Sherman. 1978. Sex-related differences in mathematics achievement, spatial visualization, and sociocultural factors. *American Educational Research Journal* 14:51–71.

Fine, M. 1986. Why urban adolescents drop into and out of public high school. *Teachers College Record* 87:393–409.

———. 1991. *Framing dropouts: Notes on the politics of an urban public high school.* Albany: State University of New York Press.

Fontana, A., and J. H. Frey. 1994. Interviewing: The art of science. In *Handbook of qualitiative research,* eds. N. K. Denzin and Y. S. Lincoln, 361–76. Newbury Park, Calif.: Sage.

Fordham, S. 1988. Racelessness as a factor in black students' school success: Pragmatic strategy or Pyrrhic victory? *Harvard Educational Review* 58:54–84.

Fordham, S., and J. Ogbu. 1986. Black students' school success: Coping with the burden of acting white. *Urban Review* 18:176–205.

Foreman, J. R., ed. 1992. *The answer book.* Urbana, Ill.: News Paper.

Foster, M. 1993. Resisting racism: Personal testimonies of African-American teachers. In *Beyond silenced voices: Class, race, and gender in United States schools,* eds. L. Weis and M. Fine, 273–88. Buffalo: State University of New York Press.

Fowler, S. 1992. Behavioral research on peer mediation and young children. College of Education Symposium, University of Illinois, Urbana-Champaign, September.

Frame, J. 1982. *To the is-land: An autobiography.* Vol. 1. Auckland: Random Century New Zealand.

Garmezy, N. 1991. Resiliency and vulnerability to adverse developmental outcomes associated with poverty. *American Behavioral Scientist* 34:416–30.

————. 1992. Resiliency and vulnerability to adverse developmental outcomes associated with poverty. In *Saving Children at Risk*, eds. T. Thompson and S. C. Hupp, 45–60. Newbury Park, Calif.: Sage.

Garmezy, N., and M. Rutter. 1983. How, why do some kids flourish against all odds? *Behavior Today* (November) 5–7.

Gaskell, J. 1985. Course enrollment in the high school: The perspective of working-class females. *Sociology of Education* 58:48–59.

Geertz, C. 1973. *The interpretation of cultures.* New York: Basic Books.

Gilbert, P. 1989. Personally (and passively) yours: Girls, literacy, and education. *Oxford Review of Education* 15:257–65.

Gilligan, C. 1982. *In a different voice: Psychological theory and women's development.* Cambridge, Mass.: Harvard University Press.

Glesne, C., and A. Peshkin. 1992. *Becoming qualitative researchers: An introduction.* White Plains, N.Y.: Longman.

Gold, R. L. 1958. Roles in sociological field observations. *Social Forces* 36:217–23.

Goldenberg, C. 1992. The limits of expectations: A case for case knowledge about teacher expectancy effects. *American Educational Research Journal* 29:517–44.

Gottfredson, L. S. 1981. Circumscription and compromise: A developmental theory of occupational aspirations. *Journal of Counseling Psychology* 28:545–79.

Gruca, J. M. 1988. The impact of college graduation on the next generation: A path analytical model. Ph.D. diss. University of Illinois, Chicago, 1988. Abstract in *Dissertation Abstracts International* 49:10A.

Harding, S. 1986. *The science question in feminism.* Ithaca, N.Y.: Cornell University Press.

————. 1991. *Whose science? Whose knowledge?: Thinking from women's lives.* Ithaca, N.Y.: Cornell University Press.

Hess, R., and S. Holloway. 1984. Family and school as educational institutions. In *Review of child development research,* ed. R. Parke, 7:179–222. Chicago: University of Chicago Press.

hooks, b. 1989. *Talking back: Thinking feminist, thinking black.* Boston: South End Press.

Hutchinson, V. 1985. *Excelling: High school superstars and how to become one.* New York: Rosen Publishing Group.

Jansen, G. 1992. Helping perspectives of South East Asian refugee women as paraprofessional helpers. Ph.D. diss. University of Illinois, Urbana-Champaign.

Kenway, J., and S. Willis. 1990. *Hearts and minds: Self-esteem and the schooling of girls.* New York: Falmer Press.

Kerr, B. A. 1985. *Smart girls, gifted women.* Columbus: Ohio Psychology Publishing.

Kessler, S., D. J. Ashenden, R. W. Connell, and G. W. Dowsett. 1985. Gender relations in secondary schooling. *Sociology of Education* 58:34–48.

Kline, B. E., and E. B. Short. 1991. Changes in emotional resilience: Gifted adolescent females. *Roeper Review* 13:118–21.

Kotlowitz, A. 1990. *There are no children here.* New York: Anchor.

Legters, N., E. McDill, and J. McPartland. 1994. Rising to the challenge: Emerging strategies for educating students at risk. Part 3. Available from *http://www.crisny.org/not-for-profit/rosta/air-pt3.htm;* INTERNET.

Lincoln, Y. S., and E. G. Guba. 1985. *Naturalistic inquiry.* Newbury Park, Calif.: Sage.

Linn, M. C., and J. S. Hyde. 1989. Gender, mathematics, and science. *Educational Researcher* 18:17–19, 22–27.

McCarthy, C. 1990. *Race and curriculum: Social inequality and the theories and politics of difference in contemporary research on schooling.* London: Falmer Press.

———. 1993. Beyond the poverty of theory in race relations: Nonsynchrony and social difference in education. In *Beyond silenced voices: Class, race, and gender in United States schools,* eds. L. Weis and M. Fine, 325–46. Buffalo: State University of New York Press.

McCaslin, M., and T. L. Good. 1992. Compliant cognition: The misalliance of management and instructional goals in current school reform. *Educational Researcher* 21:4–17.

McCutcheon, G. 1988. Curriculum and the work of teachers. In *The curriculum: Problems, politics, and possibilities,* ed. L. E. Beyer and M. Apple, 191–203. Albany, N.Y.: State University of New York Press.

McGinty, S., L. DeStefano, and S. Hasazi. n.d. *Perspectives on dropping out: Voices of special education adolescents.* Forthcoming.

McNeil, L. M. 1986. *Contradictions of control: School structure and school knowledge.* New York: Routledge.

McRobbie, A. 1978. Working class girls and the culture of femininity. In *Women take issue: Aspects of women's subordination,* ed. A. McRobbie, 96–108. Women's Study Group, Center for Contemporary Cultural Studies. London: Hutchinson.

Madhubuti, S. 1992. The new concept development school, Chicago. Paper presented at the meeting of the Program for the Study of Cultural Values and Ethics, November, Champaign, Ill.

Marston, A. R., D. F. Jacobs, R. D. Singer, K. F. Widaman, and T. D. Little. 1988. Adolescents who apparently are invulnerable to drug, alcohol, and nicotine use. *Adolescence* 23:593–98.

Middleton, S. 1987. "Streaming" and the politics of female sexuality: Case studies in the schooling of girls. In *Gender under scrutiny,* eds. G. Weiner and M. Arnot., 77–89. London: Hutchinson.

Mills, C. W. 1959. *The sociological imagination.* New York: Oxford University Press.

Mills, R. C. 1991. A new understanding of self: The role of affect, state of mind, self-understanding, and intrinsic motivation. *Journal of Experimental Education* 60:67–81.

Minnesota Women's Fund. 1990. *Reflections of risk: Growing up female in Minnesota—A report on the health and well-being of adolescent girls in Minnesota.* Minneapolis: Minnesota Women's Fund.

Mosley, E. 1992. The corporate school of Chicago. Paper presented at the meeting of the Program for the Study of Cultural Values and Ethics, November, Champaign, Ill.

Noddings, N. 1984. *Caring: A feminine approach to ethics and moral education.* Berkeley: University of California Press.

———. 1988. Schools face crisis in caring. *Education Week* (December 7):34–36.

Ogbu, J. 1991. Cultural diversity and children's learning. Paper presented at the American Educational Research Association, April, Chicago.

———. 1994. Minority status, cultural frame of reference, and schooling. In *Literacy: Interdisciplinary conversations,* ed. D. Keller-Cohen. Cresskill, N. J.: Hampton Press.

Pallas, A. M. 1984. *The determinants of high school dropout.* Ph.D. diss. Johns Hopkins University, Baltimore.

Peshkin, A. 1985. Virtuous subjectivity: In the participant observer's I's. In *Exploring clinical methods for social research,* ed. D. Berg and K. Smith, 267–82. Newbury Park, Calif.: Sage.

———. 1988. In search of subjectivity—one's own. *Educational Researcher* 17:17–22.

———. 1991. *The color of strangers, the color of friends: The play of ethnicity in school and community.* Chicago: University of Chicago Press.

———. 1992. Experiencing subjectivity. Keynote address presented at the Qualitative Research in Education Conference, January 4, Athens, Ga.

Phelan, P., A. L. Davidson, and H. T. Cao. 1991. Students' multiple worlds: Negotiating the boundaries of family, peer, and school cultures. *Anthropology and Education Quarterly* 22:224–50.

Pines, M. 1984. Resilient children: The search for protective factors. *American Educator* (fall):34–37.

Powell, A. G., E. Farrar, and D. K. Cohen. 1985. *The shopping mall high school: Winners and losers in the educational marketplace.* Boston: Houghton Mifflin.

Reinharz, S. 1992. *Feminist methods in social research.* New York: Oxford University Press.

The resilient woman: Strength in the face of adversity. 1992. Spring Foundation Symposium, January. Stanford University, Palo Alto, Calif.

Rhodes, J., and G. Blackham. 1987. Differences in character roles between adolescents from alcoholic and nonalcoholic homes. *Journal of Drug and Alcohol Abuse* 13:145–55.

Rist, R. 1970. Student social class and teacher expectations: The self-fulfilling prophecy in ghetto education. *Harvard Educational Review* 40:441–51.

Rollins, B. C., and D. L. Thomas. 1975. A theory of parental power and child compliance. In *Power in Families,* eds. R. E. Cromwell and D. H. Olson. New York: John Wiley and Sons.

Roman, L., and M. Apple. 1990. Is naturalism a move away from positivism? Materialist and feminist approaches to subjectivity in ethnographic research. In *Qualitative inquiry in education: The continuing debate,* eds. E. Eisner and A. Peshkin, 38–73. New York: Teachers College Press.

Rosenberg, M. 1974. *Conceiving the self.* Malabar, Fla: Robert E. Krieger.

Rosenthal, R., and L. Jacobson. 1968. *Pygmalion in the classroom.* New York: Holt, Rinehart and Winston.

Rossman, G. B. 1984. "I owe you one": Considerations of role and reciprocity in a study of graduate education for school administrators. *Anthropology and Education Quarterly* 15: 225–34.

Rutter, M. 1984. Resilient children. *Psychology Today* (March):57–65.

Rutter, M., B. Maughan, P. Mortimore, and J. Ouston. 1979. *Fifteen thousand hours: Secondary schools and their effects on children.* Cambridge, Mass.: Harvard University Press.

Sadker, M. P., and D. M. Sadker. 1982. *Sex equity handbook for schools.* White Plains, N.Y.: Longman.

Salzman, J. P. 1989. Save the world, save myself: Responses to problematic attachment. In *Making connections: The relational worlds of adolescent girls at Emma Willard School,* eds. C. Gilligan, N. P. Lyons, and T. J. Hanmer, 110–46. Cambridge, Mass.: Harvard University Press.

Sanjek, R., ed. 1990. *Fieldnotes: The makings of anthropology.* Ithaca, N.Y.: Cornell University Press.

School dropouts: Patterns and policies. 1986. *Teachers College Record,* 87.

Schultz D. L. 1991. *Risk, resiliency, and resistance: Current research on adolescent girls.* Ms. Foundation for Women, National Girls Initiative. New York: National Council for Research on Women.

Seligman, M. 1975. *Helplessness: On depression, development, and death.* San Francisco: W. H. Freeman.

Sewell, W., and R. Hauser. 1975. *Education, occupation, and earnings: Achievement in the early career.* New York: Academic Press.

Smith, D. E. 1987. *The everyday world as problematic: A feminist sociology.* Boston: Northeastern University Press.

Solomon, R. P. 1992. *Black resistance in high school: Forging a separatist culture.* Albany, N.Y.: State University of New York Press.

Spradley, J. P. 1980. *Participant observation.* New York: Holt, Rinehart and Winston.

Steinberg, L. 1988. *Noninstructional influence on high school student achievement: The contributions of parents, peers, extracurricular activities, and part-time work.* Madison, Wis.: National Center on Effective Secondary Schools.

Steinberg, L., J. D. Elmen, and N. S. Mounts. 1989. Authoritative parenting, psychosocial maturity, and academic success among adolescents. *Child Development* 60:1424–36.

Van Manen, M. 1990. *Researching lived experience: Human science for an action sensitive pedagogy.* London, Ont.: State University of New York Press.

Wang, M. C., and G. D. Haertel. 1995. Educational resilience. In *Handbook of special and remedial education: Research and practice,* eds. M. C. Wang, M. C. Reynolds, and H. J. Walberg, 159–91. Oxford, England: Pergamon Press.

Wax, R. 1971. *Doing fieldwork: Warning and advice*. Chicago: University of Chicago Press.

Weade, G. 1990. Gaining entry and building trust: A continuing negotiation. Paper presented at the symposium on Entry and Access in Classroom Process Research: Conceptual and Methodological Issues, American Educational Research Association, April, Boston.

Weick, A. 1992. Building a strengths perspective for social work. In *The strengths perpective in social work practice,* ed. D. Saleeby, 18–26. White Plains, N.Y.: Longman.

Weis, L. 1985a. *Between two worlds*. Boston: Routledge and Keagan Paul.

———. 1985b. "Excellence" and student class, race, and gender cultures. In *Excellence in education,* eds. P. G. Altbach, G. P. Kelly, and L. Weis, 217–32. Buffalo: Prometheus Books.

———. 1990. *Working class without work: High school students in a de-industrialized economy*. New York: Routledge.

Werner, E. 1989. High risk children in young adulthood: A longitudinal study from birth to 32 years. *American Journal of Orthopsychiatry* 59:72–81.

Werner, E., and R. Smith. 1982. *Vulnerable but invincible: A longitudinal study of resilient children and youth*. New York: McGraw-Hill.

West, C., and D. Zimmerman. 1987. Doing gender. *Gender and Society,* 1, no. 2:125–51.

Whyte, W. F., and K. K. Whyte. 1984. *Learning from the field: A guide from experience*. Beverly Hills, Calif.: Sage.

Willis, P. 1977. *Learning to labour: Why working class boys get working class jobs*. Hants, England: Saxon House.

Wilson, J., W. Weikel, and H. Rose. 1982. A comparison of nontraditional and traditional career women. *Vocational Guidance Quarterly* 31:109–17.

Wilson, K. L., and J. P. Boldizar. 1990. Gender segregation in higher education: Effects of aspirations, mathematics achievement, and income. *Sociology of Education* 63:62–74.

Index

General Editors: Joseph & Linda DeVitis

As schools struggle to redefine and restructure themselves, they need to be cognizant of the new realities of adolescents. Thus, this series of monographs and textbooks is committed to depicting the variety of adolescent cultures that exist in today's post-industrial societies. It is intended to be a primarily qualitative research, practice, and policy series devoted to contextual interpretation and analysis that encompasses a broad range of interdisciplinary critique. In addition, this series will seek to provide a pragmatic, pro-active response to the current backlash of conservatism that continues to dominate political discourse, practice, and policy. This series seeks to address issues of curriculum theory and practice; multicultural education; aggression and violence; the media and arts; school dropouts; homeless and runaway youth; alienated youth; at-risk adolescent populations; family structures and parental involvement; and race, ethnicity, class, and gender studies.

Send proposals and manuscripts to the General Editors at:

Joseph & Linda DeVitis
Binghamton University
Dept. of Education & Human Development
Binghamton, NY 13902